Daily Meditations
on the
Seven Last Words

Daily Meditations
on the
Seven Last Words

G. *George* Ernest Thomas

ABINGDON PRESS
NEW YORK   NASHVILLE

DAILY MEDITATIONS ON THE SEVEN LAST WORDS

Library of Congress Catalog Card Number: 59-5214

SET UP, PRINTED, AND BOUND BY THE
PARTHENON PRESS, AT NASHVILLE,
TENNESSEE, UNITED STATES OF AMERICA

abingdon
g.
3-13-59 agc
3-30-59 cdm

Preface

THE CROSS IS CENTRAL IN THE CHRISTIAN FAITH. THE SEVEN last words which Jesus uttered on the cross are a summary of Christian truth. They suggest what ought to be the attitudes of a follower of Jesus toward God and toward his daily obligations.

The seven weeks of meditations which are included in this book present an opportunity to look closely at the meaning of the Cross for the individual and for society. They are designed to be used as a basis for study in groups, or to be read aloud in family circles, or to be used for private reading by individual Christians.

I am grateful to my wife for her encouragement and for her patient corrections of the manuscript and to my secretary, Mrs. Ursa Worthy, for her labor in the typing.

G. ERNEST THOMAS

Contents

9

Contents

11

FIRST WEEK

"Father, Forgive Them;
For They Know Not What They Do."
—Luke 23:34

FIRST DAY

A Journey to the Cross

Scripture: Read Luke 23:1-34

OUR FAITH IS STRENGTHENED WHEN WE RECALL THE EVENTS which occurred when Jesus was crucified. The man from Nazareth had been condemned to death. The announcement of the verdict must have brought some measure of relief to those who loved him. At least the arguments before the chief priests and Pilate were finished. The plotters were through now with hypocrisy and lying. They had what they wanted.

Setting out from Pilate's judgment hall, the procession of the condemned moved slowly through the busiest streets of the city. Jesus and the two thieves who were to die with him carried the crosses on which they were to be hanged. That was part of the penalty, a humiliation arranged by the authorities to remove every vestige of arrogance from those who might have gone out to die as heroes.

Jesus staggered under the load. He was weak from fasting, from beatings, and from the lash of scorn. Even before the procession reached the Damascus gate, the Galilean staggered and fell. Soldiers quickly laid hold upon a stranger from Cyrene to bear his cross.

It was about nine o'clock when the slow-moving procession reached the summit of Calvary. The man from Galilee was stripped of his clothing, then stretched out on the ground where the cross awaited him. "The nails!" commanded the centurion sharply. Several quick blows and one hand was fastened to the crosspiece; a few more strokes and the other hand was made secure. A terse order and the feet of Jesus were pinned to the upright. More than a score of soldiers joined their strength to lift the cross from the ground. They raised it to the point where it seemed for an instant to stand motionless. "Now!" shouted the officer, pointing to the hole which had been dug in preparation. The cross dropped with relentless force, then trembled against the sky.

The body of Jesus tightened under the fearful shock of the sudden, tearing jar. Even the spectators who had come to scorn the Nazarene must have shuddered before the horror of that moment. Attention wavered momentarily while the same procedure was repeated for the two thieves. Then three crosses were silhouetted against the sky.

Their work finished—except for the formality of the death-watch—the soldiers settled down to wait for the end to come. Some of them drank; others occupied their time in gambling. They disposed of the Galilean's clothing by a roll of the dice.

Jesus had remained silent during the brutal business of crucifixion. It was customary for victims of such torture to curse, or shriek, or plead for mercy; but Jesus neither asked for release nor cried aloud. A few moments passed before he spoke for the first time. His eyes sought out the soldiers, then the representatives of the chief priests, and the disorderly crowd which was milling behind them. "Father, forgive them; for they know not what they do," he said.

Faithful Christians in every age have been moved to deep emotion and changed in outlook by the events which occurred on the first Good Friday. Life is never the same for any of us when we have made a pilgrimage to the cross.

Prayer

Eternal God, we are walking today where Jesus walked. We thank thee for the revelation of thyself in him. Before the horror of the Cross we stand in silent awe. Help us to be worthy of thy love for all thy children. In Jesus' name we pray. Amen.

SECOND DAY

The Necessity of Forgiveness

Scripture: Read Matt. 18:1-22

IT MAY SEEM STRANGE THAT THE FIRST WORD OF JESUS ON THE cross was one of forgiveness. It is easily understandable by those who are acquainted with the record of his public ministry. Jesus left no doubt in the minds of his hearers that a spirit of forgiveness is necessary if faith is to be real.

On one occasion Peter came to him. "Lord, how oft shall my brother sin against me, and I forgive him?" he asked; "till seven times?" Jesus did not hesitate. "I say not unto thee, Until seven times: but, Until seventy times seven."

In the intimacy of the close fellowship of the Master with his disciples they had raised questions concerning the meaning of prayer. They had seen Jesus return filled with new power after hours spent praying on the mountainside. They pleaded to be shown how they could receive a similar renewal of their minds and bodies. In replying to their questions, Jesus gave them a pattern for prayer which has been used by his followers in every age. No one can repeat his words without being reminded that he must forgive. "Forgive us our trespasses, as we forgive those who trespass against us," he had said. As if to remove any lingering doubt concerning the necessity for such an attitude, he added: "And when ye stand praying, forgive, if ye have aught against any; that your Father also which is in heaven may forgive you your trespasses."

The word of forgiveness from the cross was a vivid example of what Jesus had continually demanded of those who followed him. It was in keeping with his consecrated life that he never called upon his disciples to do what he would not do himself. He never pointed to a way of action, demanding that his disciples walk that path without, at the same time, living out the demands of the challenge in his own life. He not only talked of forgiveness as a necessary attribute of a godly life, but he exemplified that spirit by his willing forgiveness of those whose hatred had brought him to his death.

Many Christians easily dismiss the demand for a forgiving spirit by saying that they have no enemies in the sense that Jesus had enemies. "There are some people whom I dislike, but none whom I really hate," said a young woman who was struggling to make faith a vital factor in her life. Her pride might have suffered a blow if her thoughts had gone beyond her relatives and her immediate circle of friends. Sometimes hatred is directed against people of different nationalities. We seldom, if ever, come into personal contact with such an indefinite group. There are few opportunities to practice the virtue of forgiveness of those who live on the other side of the world. Too often we use such reasoning to justify our attitudes as we mumble the words of forgiveness in the Lord's Prayer.

It is always easier to do a single heroic deed than to main-

18

tain a high level of Christian devotion in our daily contacts with those about us. The attitude of forgiveness demands something of us in our day-by-day relationships in the family and in the community. When we carry resentment against our brother or our neighbor, we are as great a traitor to Christ as is the man who despises the people on the other side of the world. The Cross is an eternal challenge to us to forgive.

Prayer

Help us to forgive, O God. Save us from petty jealousies and envies. Keep us from the temptation to hide our own weaknesses by blaming others. May the spirit of the Christ who was willing to pardon his enemies fill our hearts until all malice and hatred have been removed. Give us strength to love the unlovely and to care for the unworthy. In Jesus' name. Amen.

THIRD DAY

Hatred as a Spiritual Barrier

Scripture: Read Matt. 5:38-48

HATRED AND RESENTMENT LEAVE THEIR MARK, NOT ALONE upon our relationship with God, but upon our habits and outlooks as well. Charles M. Campbell of Harvard University describes the conflicts which arise when forgiveness becomes a lost art.

It is astonishing to notice that individuals, who keep careful watch on their blood-pressure, on their weight, on their digestive apparatus, may have little interest in their inequality of temper,

19

their unreasonable and obscure behavior, the unnatural domestic situations which are partly the product of their own personality. The father of a family may consult regularly his family physician to make sure his blood-pressure is in good order, but does not mention to the physician that for years he has not been on speaking terms with his own son.[1]

Jesus was aware that such weaknesses are a common failing of people in every walk of life. Matthew said of him that he knew what was in the human heart. Indeed he did! He was aware that violent hatred erects a barrier, not only between a man and the one he hates, but between a man and his God.

A classic incident is told of King Albert of Belgium. On one of his many visits to the war front during World War I he passed through a recently bombed town. A small group of children had gathered about a roadside shrine to ask for divine help in the hour when destruction and death had robbed them of everything except life itself. They were repeating the Lord's prayer: "Forgive us our trespasses, as we . . ." There the voices hesitated and stopped. The eldest in the group tried to make the children go on: "I know, I know, but we *must* say the prayer. 'Forgive those . . .'" She stopped, and then another voice took up her words: "As we forgive those who trespass against us." It was King Albert, standing close by, unseen by the praying children. King Albert was willing to forgive, yet he went away from that roadside shrine to inspire his people to further deeds of bravery against the foe. His earnest prayer for forgiveness did not blind him to greed and injustice, nor did it lessen his resolution to do all in his power to right such wrongs.

[1] *A Present-day Conception of Mental Disorders* (Cambridge: Harvard University Press, 1924), pp. 17-18.

A Pennsylvania community faced a tragedy when the only bank in the town closed its doors. The president of the institution was arrested and charged with the theft of nearly a million dollars. The whole town was affected. Hundreds of depositors were threatened with the loss of their life savings. In that hour it was natural that their anger should be turned against the person who had robbed them. But soon the citizens of the town began to remember the man's kindness on many occasions when people had been unable to pay back money which had been borrowed. They recalled his generosity to causes which looked toward the improvement of the town. Like a wave moving in from the sea, the call for forgiveness was heard on every hand. The people recognized that the man must pay the penalty exacted by the law, but they united their voices to ask for mercy. They were willing to forgive.

The voice of Jesus from the cross offered forgiveness to those whose greed and hatred had brought him to that hour of agony. The one who had always been ready to pardon the evildoer, while still striking firmly against the evil, exemplified his teachings to the very end. He did not waver even when suffering the agonies of crucifixion. In his example we will always hear God's challenge to us to love one another.

Prayer

Save us, O Lord, from the hatred which would possess us, lest we lose our knowledge of thee. Forgive us the sins of hate which drive us to scorn of our fellow men. Help us to love one another as thou dost love us. In Jesus' name. Amen.

A Reason to Forgive

Scripture: Read Matt. 6:1-15

"THEY KNOW NOT WHAT THEY DO," JESUS SAID, EXPLAINING the reason for his willingness to forgive. Strange, is it not? The Roman centurion and his legionnaires knew they were servants of the state bringing death to an innocent man. The chief priests had learned the significance of his mission from the lips of Jesus himself; they should have known what they were about. The mob was made up of common people like those who had once "heard him gladly"; they must have realized what was involved. Yet Jesus declared that they did not know what they were doing.

If the groups which brought the Master to the cross were unaware of their mistake, how much more claim to innocence have many of the people whom we treat harshly and whom we refuse to forgive. "They know not what they do." These words should be recalled when a member of the family has incurred anger and hatred because of his selfishness. They should be repeated when race prejudice or international tensions have led us into a habit of thinking which can only result in a deep, fixed hatred.

A story is told about Henriette Sontag, a celebrated European singer, who was forced to overcome numerous obstacles in her struggle for success. Not the least of these hardships resulted from the opposition of Amelia Steininger, a competitor. Everywhere Sontag went, she suffered from the persecution of her rival. The quiet of a hall in which she was singing was broken by the hisses and catcalls of those hired to halt the concert. Wherever she went, gossip started by Steininger made life difficult. Posters announcing her appearances were torn down or disfigured. But Sontag refused to strike back. And, in the end, her beautiful voice won the acclaim which she so richly deserved.

Many years later Sontag noticed a little girl leading a blind woman down a street in Berlin. She recognized the blind beggar as her former rival. She made herself known, took care of Steininger's needs, and offered her friendship. When someone asked Sontag how she had been able to demonstrate such kindness to the one who had done so much to make her life difficult, she replied: "She didn't realize what she was doing."

We react quickly in moments when we sense a personal affront. We forget that selfishness often distorts the outlook of a friend who needs, at that time, not so much to be hated as to be understood. The longing for social approval frequently leads a loved one or an associate to deeds which, in a later moment, will seem as distasteful to him as to the one who is injured. We must endeavor to approach the problem with the knowledge that "they know not what they do."

The earthly ministry of Jesus reached new heights in the word of forgiveness. His example forever challenges us. We are still bewildered to know how we can purge our minds of the deep, fixed animosities which tend to warp our outlook, which keep us tossing sleeplessly at night, and which lead us to make quick retorts in answer to charges unfairly leveled against us. The example of Jesus is etched clearly in our minds. He looked into the faces of those whose greed and selfishness had brought him to that hour of suffering. "Father, forgive them; for they know not what they do," he said.

These words of forgiveness will haunt men and women until the end of time. We can never be satisfied until we too learn how to forgive.

Prayer

Teach us, O Lord, thy will. May the Spirit of Christ purge our minds of all that is unworthy. Help us to see the good in others and the evil in ourselves. Give us courage to love as thou dost love. In Jesus' name. Amen.

FIFTH DAY

God Forgives

Scripture: Read Acts 7:54-60

JESUS SUFFERED ON THE CROSS AS ANY VICTIM OF THAT INHUMAN type of torture suffered. He felt all the physical pain which others had felt before him. Some of the "words" which he spoke on Calvary reflect the strain which crucifixion placed upon his physical body. His first recorded comment, "Father, forgive them; for they know not what they do," offers an unforgettable portrait of Christianity at work in a hostile world. There is a matchless grandeur in the Cross in spite of the fact that it tore every vestige of decency from its victims and made them subject to all the weaknesses of the flesh.

Strange as it may seem, Christ broke through the preparations which had been made to hold him up to scorn. When the end finally came, the centurion summed up the experience of those hours by saying, "Surely, he was the son of God." Many others in the crowd must have felt that the centurion had spoken for them.

Not only was it the son of Mary, but also the son of God, who died upon the cross. The words of Jesus are not merely the voice of the greatest man who ever lived, but the eternal message of one who has a significance beyond the human. Let no one forget that it was a divine voice which whispered the Seven Last Words.

Understood from this point of view, the word of forgiveness reveals truth about the nature of God which offers hope for all mankind. "Father, forgive them; for they know not what they do," he said. To catch the full meaning of these words is to discover hidden depths in the love of God.

God forgives! That is the inevitable conclusion when we hear what Jesus is saying. The nature of the heavenly Father is brought into clearer focus. The picture is one of a God who offers pardon to the worst of men. The men who plotted infamy were there; the men who carried out the orders and actually committed the deed were there; the people who either stood silent or joined in scornful shouts were there. The men in that company typify the human failure of all the ages. It was they who were forgiven by the mercy of the one whom they sought to destroy.

The Old Testament reveals only faint glimpses of a forgiving God. Certain obligations had been placed upon humanity by the divine act of creation. When men broke the laws of Jehovah, he turned upon them in righteous indignation and anger. The earliest conception of forgiveness required men to remove the cause of the offense. Jehovah would then look once again upon the people and be gracious to them. If we mean by forgiveness the restoration of the offender, without obligation or price, to the freedom which he has forfeited, then we must admit that there is no forgiveness in the Law.

The prophets declared that God would forgive sin and evil, but they were certain he meted out punishment to the third and fourth generations of those who transgressed his laws.

The words of Jesus from the cross give assurance that the heavenly Father is willing to bestow a greater measure of mercy than mankind had ever known. He demands nothing; he bargains not at all; he makes no exceptions. God was speaking through Jesus. His voice offers unlimited forgiveness to all of us, however unworthy we may be.

Prayer

We praise thee, O God, for thy creating and sustaining power. We give thanks that thou art our Father, available to all thy children who seek thy presence. Most of all, we claim the gift of thy love. We are not worthy to be forgiven of our sins, but we gladly accept the promise which was made perfect on the cross. Help us to live as those who are aware of thy mercies. In Jesus' name. Amen.

SIXTH DAY

A Key to the Nature of God

Scripture: Read I Cor. 13

IT IS UNDERSTANDABLE WHY WE SHOULD IDENTIFY THE SPIRIT of Christ with the nature of God. We could not believe that Jesus was greater in his mercy than was his heavenly Father. "The cross of Christ is not the means of procuring forgive-

ness," said Henry Sloane Coffin; "the Father waits to be
gracious." [2] Christ's forgiveness uncovered the sympathetic
heartbeat of Almighty God.

A feeling of awe grips and holds us when we stand before
this matchless picture of divine love in action. The poet
Heinrich Heine said, "Of course God will forgive us. That is
his job: what is God for?" No such blatant arrogance satisfies
one who has seen the heart of the Eternal reflected in the
words of Christ. It is a gift beyond measure.

Followers of Jesus who had walked with him down the
Galilean road had already grasped a partial understanding of
the nature of a loving and forgiving God. They had listened
to the Master as he unfolded the story of the prodigal son
who, straying far from his father's home and heart, found when
he returned not merely a welcome, but arms which longed to
enfold him and eyes which had grown weary from watching
the road down which he had hoped the wanderer would come.

The parable of the prodigal son may have been a subject
of speculation for many of his listeners. "It's too good to be
true," they must have said. They had heard too often the
voices of those who reminded them that every sin requires a
blood offering to accept easily the idea of a forgiving God.

Their doubts were resolved on Calvary. The body of Jesus
suffered all the torture which man could fashion. In that hour
he spoke words of forgiveness: "Father, forgive them; for they
know not what they do." The voice reflected the heart of God.
It promised new hope for a tired and discouraged world. It
told men that it is the nature of God to forgive!

Words have weight in proportion to the place where they
originate. The words of a politician who makes promises to

[2] *The Meaning of the Cross* (New York: Charles Scribner's Sons, 1931),
p. 121.

the electorate are always discounted by the knowledge that he is campaigning for office. The words of a newspaper columnist are understood in the light of the pressure placed upon him to produce a sensational story. The Cross was stark reality. The words which Jesus uttered while suffering intense pain assume a significance for all the ages.

Men in desperate need turn to the crucified Christ for an answer to the longings of their hearts. He reveals the eternal God as a forgiving father. It is a truth which lifts the despair of all mankind.

John Erskine, famous writer and educator, felt for many years that he was estranged from God. He tried without success to find a way to break the veil which separated him from the divine Being. He often referred to the dumbness of God. He prayed and thought he heard no answering voice. "If only he could speak to me so that I might hear!" he cried. But one day he found the answer to his longings. "Once God spoke," he declared. "It was on Calvary." Erskine heard the voice from the cross and knew God cared for him.

The willingness of God to forgive our evil deeds is still an eternal mystery. The word of forgiveness from the lips of Jesus gives reality to the hope. His words reflect the nature of the heavenly Father. They promise that God is ready to forgive!

Prayer

We come to thee, O Lord, not with an awareness of our merits, but with a consciousness of our needs. Help us to forgive as we are forgiven. Enable us to understand the depth of thy love as it was revealed on Calvary. We claim the assurances which were made real on the cross. In Jesus' name. Amen.

SEVENTH DAY

The Demands of Divine Forgiveness
Scripture: Read John 17:11-26

THERE ARE SOME WHO QUESTION THE WISDOM OF GOD IN MAK-
ing an offer of free pardon such as Jesus made on the cross.
We understand it while our eyes are fixed upon the crucified
Christ. But when our gaze strays to the harsh and cruel faces
of those to whom the miracle is extended, we are mystified. "Is
there no demand for a changed heart and a changed life before
the gift of forgiveness is granted?" we ask.

Leaders in Hinduism and Buddhism have charged that the
Christian doctrine of forgiveness is lacking in moral firmness.
They declare that the oriental doctrine of karma has a better
sense of justice when it holds that through successive incarna-
tions men build up a character which, at every stage, suffers
exactly what is appropriate to fit its evil deeds.

Christ's word of forgiveness did not assume that men would
remain unchanged. He dared to peer into the future with hope
that his example and suffering would bring a transformation in
the attitudes of men. He looked forward to the conquest of
evil by the irresistible example of the Cross.

We would never be entirely satisfied with a God who looks
with tolerance upon the shoddy mistakes which we make every
day. If God were to say "never mind" to our confessions of
failure, if our dishonesty and hatred merely brought from him
a mild reminder that we need not concern ourselves about it,

then moral grandeur would be lost from the universe. If "Father, forgive them; . . ." meant nothing more than a weak tolerance of wickedness, we would turn from a God who was less admirable than Old Testament concepts of a Jehovah who ruled the world with sternness.

God's mercy is greater than that! We stand once more with the people who are looking up at the cross. We are a part of the crowd because we too have failed to achieve the best we know and have faltered when faced with choices between right and wrong. Once again we listen intently to the word of forgiveness. It is a wondrous experience, but there is more to it than a feeling of relief because we are pardoned. When we accept the miracle which is offered on Calvary, we cannot go back to the old way of life. Not even if we try, we can't. We feel strange stirrings within which make evil choices forever difficult. We are caught up by a challenge to follow Christ. Sometimes we fail, but always we are aware that we have failed, and we start again with fresh determination to live more nobly in the days ahead. To be forgiven does not prompt us to lead smug or complacent lives. It marks the beginning of new purposes and resolutions. We can never be content until we are striving to let Christ's spirit shine through us.

Prayer

We give thanks unto thee, O God, for the words of forgiveness which Jesus uttered on the cross. In Christ we see thee. Our unworthiness of such love lies heavy upon us. We have failed thee again and again. Yet we dare to claim thy promise. Forgive us! Help us to live by the light of that faith. In Jesus' name. Amen.

SECOND WEEK

"To day Shalt Thou Be with Me in Paradise"

—*Luke 23:43*

FIRST DAY

Hope for All of Humanity

Scripture: Read Luke 23:35-45

TRADITION HAS INDICATED THAT THE THREE CROSSES ON CALVARY formed a semicircle. Jesus of Nazareth hung in the center; the two thieves were at his right and left, yet far enough in front of him so they were able to gaze at each other and at him. It was a clever strategy to torture the victims by allowing them to see in others the degradation to which they themselves had been brought.

As the moments passed, the silence which had fallen over the onlookers while the act of crucifixion was being carried out gave way to taunts. The chief priests pushed their way to the front ranks. Their words tell us that, even with the Galilean hanging on the cross, they were not certain that they had disposed of him. "This fellow saved others," they shouted to the crowd: "Let him save himself if he is God's anointed, the chosen one."

Encouraged by the ridicule heaped upon Jesus by the high officials, the soldiers "made sport of him." One of them offered him sour wine. "Are you the king of the Jews?" he cried. "Save yourself then!"

Jesus did not answer. At that moment the focus of attention shifted from the central cross to those who were hanging with him.

Two thieves! Little is known of their background or offenses, save only this: one victim admitted they were guilty of the crimes which had led to their conviction. "We are indeed suffering justly," he said, "for we are receiving due requital for what we have done." We do not know whether they were Galileans, Judeans, Samaritans, or from one of the far provinces. They had been caught in crimes which were punishable by death.

One of the thieves added his scorn to those of the crowd. He spoke insultingly: "Are you not the Christ? Save yourself and us." He expected no help. Perhaps he hoped to ease his torture by heaping ridicule upon the one who was a victim with him.

The kind of affront to God in which men mouth a prayer, but expect no response, is often heard among those whose faith has ebbed away. It was the insulting cry of a young mother who was close to death. "Why don't you call upon your God?" she cried; "maybe he isn't there." God may have been straining at that moment to help her, but she would have nothing to do with him. Her mind was set in a pattern of doubt.

Much of the seeming lack of response to prayer is explained by the doubts in the mind of the one who prays. The skeptic may say, "Save thyself and us," but the words are a mockery because he does not expect God to help him.

The other thief responded with words of rebuke. Something had happened in the short hours since he was dragged before the tribunal and there sentenced to death. Perhaps it began when he observed Christ's calm demeanor before Pilate, answering the charges against him so effectively that only a greed for popular favor could have allowed the Roman to make such a travesty of justice. The change may have come during the long journey to the summit of Calvary. The thief had found time to turn his eyes toward the strange man who was the central figure in the procession. Perhaps the change came when Jesus spoke the word of forgiveness.

This criminal silenced the cries of the one on the other side of Jesus. He did not claim innocence, nor did he attempt to throw the blame for their plight upon others. "We indeed are suffering justly, for we are receiving due requital." Then his head turned slowly so he could look into the face of Christ.

"Jesus, remember me when you come into your kingdom," he pleaded.

The narrative in Luke indicates that the Master replied immediately. He took no time to contemplate the proper answer. His response was direct and clear.

"I tell you a solemn truth," Jesus said. "Today shalt thou be with me in paradise."

These words are startling. They seem at first a denial of divine justice. But listen again. Think what the words mean to each of us. There is hope here beyond all our dreams.

Prayer

There is mystery in the cross, O thou our God. Help us to understand thy truth. May we walk lightly this day, knowing that eternity is only one step away. Give us faith to live out our destiny as thy children. Help us to walk in the light of the purpose thou hast for each of us. In Jesus' name. Amen.

A God Whom Men Can Trust

Scripture: Read John 14:1-14

MANY DIFFERENT TRUTHS ARE SUGGESTED BY THE CALM assertion which Jesus made to the thief that day on Calvary. There is enough here upon which to build a faith for all eternity.

We are impressed by the unwavering trust in God which the words suggest. Jesus was hanging on a cross. He was subject to all the fears which have haunted men across the ages. He might easily have decided that the world was awry and life had no purpose. "Today shalt thou be with me in paradise" offers hope for the lost of the ages, but more than that it declares Jesus' confidence in a divine plan. His faith in God and in the heavenly Father's purpose was unshaken.

All of us are tossed about like a ship without a rudder when we no longer trust the providence of God. Unless we can assert our confident faith in the plans and purposes of a heavenly Father, it takes far less than a cross to break our spirits. We easily become despondent when our schemes are frustrated or when nature's provision for our needs is not precisely what we anticipated it would be. Many a farmer has planted his fields with expectation that the rains and sunshine would be favorable and has left no room for the possibility that there might be several weeks of dry weather. The half a crop which resulted became a reason for him to doubt God's goodness.

Many a businessman has begun to question God's mercy because the stock market did not rise as fast as he had anticipated it would. Cynicism and doubt are inevitable results of a misdirected faith.

Jesus was suffering humanity's supreme disgrace. As a means of torture the cross had no equal among the instruments designed by men to inflict pain upon other human beings. The Second Word lets us look into the heart of Christ. We find no bitterness, no uncertainty. God remains the supreme fact in his life. He has confidence that divine purposes will triumph even before the day comes to an end.

Sensitive souls in the crowd must have lifted their heads a little higher in hope when these words were spoken. They were looking at a man who ought to have been broken in spirit, but who wasn't. And why? Because he believed in God and was confident that the divine will was able to triumph over the worst which could happen.

Some people never reach the place where trust in God enables them to conquer disapointment and defeat. They live to the end of their days without discovering what it means to receive divine help in an hour of need.

Matthew Arnold has said:

> With heads bent o'er their toil, they languidly
> Their lives to some unmeaning taskwork give,
> Dreaming of naught beyond their prison wall.
> And as, year after year,
> Fresh products of their barren labour fall
> From their tired hands, . . .
>
> .   .   .   .
>
> Death in their prison reaches them
> Unfreed, having seen nothing, still unblest.[1]

[1] From "A Summer Night."

The prison house of doubt holds countless victims. Many of us go our busy, hurried way without pausing to discover the source of eternal life. We are too absorbed in that which is transient to glimpse the truths which are everlasting.

The words of Jesus to the thief—"Today shalt thou be with me in paradise"—hold many promises for humanity. Best of all, they remind us that we have a God whom we can confidently trust, even in the midst of life's defeats.

Prayer

We thank thee, O God, that thou art a living presence in the lives of those who trust thee. Forgive us for the doubts which rob us of our true heritage. Help us this day to breathe every breath and walk every step with the knowledge that thou art sustaining us. Deepen our faith and our trust. In Jesus' name. Amen.

THIRD DAY

The Hidden Glory in Men

Scripture: Read John 6:35-51

JESUS HAD LITTLE IN COMMON WITH THE THIEVES WHO WERE crucified with him—except a common way of dying. His life had been directed toward purposes which were the opposite of those which had driven them. He had given his life to save humanity; they had used their time and efforts to prey upon and victimize the innocent. The gulf between the Master and the thieves seemed too wide to be bridged. Yet Jesus came so close in fellowship with the repentant thief that he could give him the assurance of a destiny which they would share together.

There is a rebuke here for those of us who erect barriers between ourselves and our fellow men. We should tread lightly when we are tempted to scorn some individual or class as unworthy of our interest and fellowship. They have possibilities far greater than could have been expected of the thief.

It was one of the crowning attributes of Jesus' life that he was able to sense the hidden possibilities in men and women. Try to imagine yourself choosing Peter, James, John, and the other disciples to carry on a movement which would be world wide and ageless. Try to think of yourself as seeing virtue in Mary Magdalene if you came upon her crouching helplessly, waiting for stones to be hurled at her. Not a pretty sight and not a character which offered much hope of transformation. Jesus saw the potential goodness. History has demonstrated that his faith was justified.

How desperately we need a sensitiveness to the needs and possibilities of the unfortunate and the dispossessed! A pioneer preacher took time out in a raging snowstorm to remind a freckled-faced, red-haired country boy that he had a life to live for God. "There's just you and I here," he said, "but I have seen the world out yonder and I know that if you'll let God use your life, you can accomplish great things for him." The lad never forgot the challenge. He set a goal of service for his life, and when he had reached it, all the world paid him homage as one of the great religious leaders of his generation.

The eyes of Jesus sought out the thief who had asked for mercy. He offered the greatest hope which any individual— rich or poor, saint or sinner—could crave. "Today shalt thou be with me in paradise."

Humanity draws closer together when it stands before the

cross. Jesus had forgiven the men who had maligned and tortured him. After that he opened the doors of eternity to one who was a confessed criminal. Every Christian may appropriately ask, "How can we be narrow and bigoted and self-righteous in the presence of the Christ?"

The unforgettable message which comes from the breathless hours on Calvary is that there is hope for every man. Are there any whom we can despise when, in God's providence, they may be worthy of a place in the eternal city? We tremble before the danger of what may happen if our hatreds deprive us of God's greatest gift, while the one we loathe may find a joyous welcome from a merciful God.

It is serious business to be a Christian. The Second Word is both a supreme reason for confidence in a divine plan for the world and a challenge for us to follow Christ's example. The dying thief typifies all the failure and sin in human history. Christ calls forth our best in sympathetic understanding and love for those whose lives make them seem unworthy of confidence and trust.

Prayer

Dear Father of all minkind, forgive us for our blindness to the possibilities of those about us. Help us to see the goodness in the worst of men. Use us to stir the hidden treasures in all thy children. Make us worthy witnesses for the Christ who can make all men into new persons. In Jesus' name. Amen.

FOURTH DAY

Hope Made Eternal

Scripture: Read John 16:12-28

MORE HOPE FOR HUMANITY IS CRAMMED INTO THE SECOND Word of Jesus from the cross than in any other words ever uttered. They must have been breath-taking for the thief who heard them; they still are a doorway of hope for victims of sordid desires and unworthy deeds.

It would appear physically impossible for any individual to assume a commanding attitude while hanging on a cross. But we sense a ringing triumph in the words of Jesus: "Today shalt thou be with me in paradise." There was no temporizing here! A man had asked for mercy. He was not a good man. Death was the deserved punishment for the crimes which he had committed against society. "Remember me when thou comest into thy kingdom," he had pleaded. When Jesus answered, he left no question about the thief's destiny. Before the evening shadows fell that day, he was to walk through the gates of heaven.

The words of Jesus were a fulfillment of the mission which the Old Testament writers had pictured for the Messiah and from which Jesus did not turn away during his public ministry. He came to redeem men from sin. He revealed a God who offered salvation to all who were willing to accept it. "I am come to seek and to save that which was lost," he had said.

41

His teachings throb with references to lost coins, lost sheep, and lost souls.

There is a dramatic quality in the words spoken on the cross which is not surpassed at any other point in the Gospels. The thief was so evidently an evil man; the hour was so late. How could he or those who watched the scene expect a condemned criminal to be lifted from that place of torture to the victory which faith offers? Yet it happened! Faith won out that day, and the mountain peaks of hope for all humanity pushed up higher than ever before in history.

The human and the divine were closely linked on Calvary. The sufferings of the physical body called out human cries of anguish. Jesus was also—in a unique way—the Son of God. It is a divine voice which is speaking so eloquently in the promise of deliverance to the thief. God spoke through Christ that day. The message is one to make the heart of every victim of sin beat faster with hope. It satisfies the unspoken longings of all who eagerly await the assurance that they are not forever lost.

These words challenge every follower of Jesus to be a witness for Christ. There are countless thousands of men and women who are blind to God. They take pride in their evil deeds. At certain moments they feel dissatisfied with the pattern of their lives. They sense an emptiness in the pleasure and power for which they have struggled so desperately. Our privilege and duty is to tell them the good news. There is still time to return to God. Eternity is at stake.

Prayer

We thank thee, O God, that thy mercy is without measure. Forgive us for our sins. Set us on the way everlasting. Make us witnesses of the salvation which is able to bring every man and woman to thee. In Jesus' name. Amen.

FIFTH DAY

The Limitless Grace of God
Scripture: Read John 17:1-21

THE MESSAGE OF THE SECOND WORD IS BROAD AND INCLUSIVE. It leaves the listener with the unmistakable conclusion that men are made for immortality. To look into the face of Christ is to learn how innate goodness is and how unnatural is a life of evil.

If our weaknesses and failures lead us to identify ourselves with the repentant thief, then we may also identify our hope with his. If the tender mercy of God was extended to him, it is certain that it will be extended to us.

This sharply etched picture of a man's discovery of salvation leaves little room for arguments that the soul's return to the feet of God requires herculean efforts on the part of man. The thief did not need to follow harsh disciplines in order to qualify for the eternal life. The way to God's presence was unhampered by difficult or impassable hurdles. He had only to turn his eyes to Jesus, acknowledge Christ's power, and give evidence that he longed to be saved.

Many eloquent interpreters of spiritual reality describe religion as a struggle. For them the discovery of truth is always the result of a gallant crusade. The word of Jesus to the thief indicates that the gift of divine mercy and forgiveness is free.

43

God's grace is limitless and is meted out far beyond what we deserve.

Holy men of many religions have believed that the way to peace is to be found by torturing their bodies. Sometimes the object of the self-imposed pain was to break the hold of the body over the spirit, but more often it was an endeavor to demonstrate to a harsh and cruel God that they were worthy of his attention and concern. Such men went apart from the world to live out their days in lonely solitude; or they wore hair shirts, slept on stone floors, or subsisted on a starvation diet.

Such attempts to win the favor of God have led millions of ordinary people to despair that they can experience a consciousness of the eternal presence in their lives. It is impossible for them to go apart from the world and endure privations. They have work to do and family responsibilities to face. Even in the twentieth century there are many who still believe they can gain merit from an unfriendly God by subjecting themselves to stern discipline.

There is assurance in Christ's words to the thief. We now know that God is waiting for a sign from those of us who have failed. When we are repentant and eager for his eternal gifts, he then acts with love and mercy.

Our daily disciplines of prayer and reading the Bible are important. Indeed, they are essential if we are to keep close to God. But disciplines by themselves have no merit in the sight of God. The way to his presence is wide open. Each of us is privileged to enter as we earnestly confess our sins and welcome him into our lives.

Prayer

Save us this day, O God, from the temptation to believe that thou art far away. Help us to know that our desire for thee is matched by thy desire for us. Come into our hearts and possess our lives. In Jesus' name. Amen.

SIXTH DAY

The Miracle of God's Love

Scripture: Read Acts 26:1-23

WE DO NOT KNOW THE NATIONALITY OF THE THIEF WHO WAS promised immortality that day on Calvary. Was he Jew or Greek or Parthian? Was he slave or free? History offers no answer. The man is identified merely as a thief. Those who heard the promise must have understood that it made no difference what his national, social, or racial background might be. The gift of God's mercy did not depend upon one's being a strict Jew. It seems absurd to ask whether God would inquire concerning a man's heritage before he offered the promise of salvation.

These words of Jesus have meaning for people of every class, nationality, and race. Man-made and artificial barriers break down before the miracle of the Cross. The hope of forgiveness is for all men in every age.

Our colossal pride must often seem an affront to God. We thank God that we are not as other men are. When we bow before the cross, our failures stand out in bold silhouette. There is no room for narrowness or bigotry in the presence of the crucified Christ. If the penitent thief is at home with God, there is no one—no one—who is excluded.

"Today." A miracle is suggested by that word! Men who had speculated about the eternal life were satisfied to let the dead sleep until an hour of general awakening. The valley of Kidron, outside the walls of Jerusalem, was a burial ground which reminded those who passed by of the hope in Jewish hearts that God might someday call the dead to life. At certain periods in their history the people had wistful longings that the time of awakening might be close at hand. Usually, however, the most pious followers of Judaism were satisfied to consign their dead to the grave without hope that they would witness a resurrection.

Jesus blessed the dying thief. He offered him a destiny which was to begin before nightfall. "Today shalt thou be with me in paradise," he said.

Thousands of spectators make their way every year to planetariums to look with wonder upon the order and majesty of the heavens. They discover that the earth is not a fixed point around which all the rest of the universe revolves. The earth is seen as a tiny part of a constellation which extends beyond the sight of man. At the cross men found that time is not fixed. It flows directly into eternity.

It is characteristic of human nature for us to grasp at crumbs of knowledge which can be substantiated by our own experience. Jesus' words give authority to the belief that the eternal life for the repentant thief began when his sufferings on the cross were ended.

I was called during the night to the bedside of a young woman who was close to death. Only a few days before she had been healthy, vigorous, and strong. Now the end was at hand. She turned to her loved ones: "Good-by to all of you," she whispered; "don't grieve for me. I'm going to be with God." She went out of the earthly life singing "God Will Take Care of You," leaving behind witnesses who caught something of her confident hope. They watched as she approached the eternal life and saw that she was no longer afraid.

When Jesus said "today," he was boldly declaring that the eternal life begins immediately. This faith, discovered again by men and women in our generation, makes death a step toward victory rather than a sad ending to an incomplete life. Death is only another milestone on a pilgrimage which stretches into eternity. It is not the end; but the continuance of an existence in which God has an interest and concern.

Prayer

We thank thee, O God, for the eternal hope in our hearts which was answered by the words of Christ. Help us to live our daily lives in such a way that, when the end comes, we too shall hear the promise "Today shalt thou be with me in paradise." In Jesus' name. Amen.

SEVENTH DAY

A Foretaste of the Eternal Life

Scripture: Read I Cor. 15:34-58

THE REPENTANT THIEF FOUND A HOME. HIS LIFE AS A CRIMINAL had deprived him of a place of security or a refuge after a day's work. Now, at last, he had a resting place.

Men have speculated in every century about the meaning of the word "paradise." Where was it that the dying thief was going? Does it mean the same as Heaven? Canon F. W. Farrar declared that paradise is "where God is." That's as good a definition as any. The thief was not lost any longer. He had found a home and a loving father at the end of the road.

47

The picture here of a human soul—held down by the weaknesses of the flesh—walking triumphantly into a victorious future life has hope in it for every seeker after eternal reality. This is God's plan graphically unfolded. It is a glorious foretaste of what can become the final goal of any life.

Too much attention should not be centered on the word "paradise." It is a human characteristic that we focus our interest on that which seems more immediately satisfying while missing truth which is of greater signifiance. Jesus said, "Thou shalt be *with me* in paradise."

Whether we call the ultimate goal of the eternal life paradise or heaven is insignificant compared to the promise that the eager seeker will be with the Master.

To be where Christ is, where God is—that is the fullest answer to human hopes. The longing for streets of gold or for mansions of majestic grandeur is an empty satisfaction when compared with the anticipation that the eternal life will be lived in the presence of Christ.

The dying thief was given that assurance. He must have been no longer afraid. The pain of crucifixion did not seem so devastating; death did not stand out so starkly final.

The promise of Jesus is extended to every seeker who longs for divine certainty and peace. To each of us death is not the end, but the doorway into a new life, one in which we will have fellowship with Christ. That assurance was made clear by what happened on Calvary.

Prayer

Thy promises, O God, are our hope. Without faith in thee we would wander the earth as strangers who are lost. Forgive us for all we have done which makes us unworthy to be thy children. Give us the strength to do thy will and hope at the end of the road. In the name of Jesus we pray. Amen.

THIRD WEEK

"Woman, Behold Thy Son! ...
Behold Thy Mother!"
— *John 19:26-27*

FIRST DAY

A Concern for the Family

Scripture: Read John 19:13-27

THE MOB HAD ITS WAY ON THE DAY OF THE CRUCIFIXION. IN the sea of faces which stared up at the cross the desire for revenge was clearly in evidence. Even those who, on other occasions, might have raised their voices in a plea for mercy were caught up by the tide of fury. They too cried out for the death of the innocent.

Justice seldom triumphs when a crowd is swept along by mass hysteria. The people of Smyrna forgot their affection for Bishop Polycarp when the urge to kill changed them into a wild mob applauding the death of the one they had loved. The French Revolution became a ghastly spectacle when the rabble thirsted for the heads of the innocent and guilty alike. It is often so. The actions of the crowd on Calvary give an eloquent warning of the danger which occurs when groups of men are bent on getting their way without regard to what is right.

At least four of the people in the crowd had been in the small company of his followers and friends. "Now there stood by the cross of Jesus his mother, and his mother's sister, Mary, the wife of Cleophas, and Mary Magdalene. . . . Jesus . . . saw . . . the disciple standing by, whom he loved . . . ." The rest of the disciples were probably hiding in the shadowy byways of Jerusalem, hoping they would not be recognized as followers of the Nazarene. The common people who had "heard

51

him gladly" were either busy about other duties or had been carried along by the wave of hatred. They were almost convinced that they had been deceived when they felt the strange pull of Christ.

Mary the mother of Jesus was suffering that day as never before in her life. Her sister must have tried to dissuade her from going to Calvary. She probably felt that the tragic sight was not meant for a mother's eyes. When Mary had insisted that she must remain close to her son, her sister had gone with her to help bear the grief.

This mother had loved her first-born son with an affection which never could be given to another. He must have been a helpful and loving boy. His work in the carpenter's shop had won the approval of the neighbors. Mary was proud of him. Yet when he reached manhood, she found it difficult to understand him. He spent more time than other young men out on the hillside, sometimes under the stars. He studied the books of the Law and the Prophets as if he were a leader in the synagogue. Often he expressed ideas which she knew would be dangerous if they were uttered outside the family circle.

She had followed the crowd many times during the brief months when his popularity was the topic of conversation wherever people met. But she had been quick to sense the growing opposition of the organized religious forces. She had spent many a sleepless night wondering how it all was to end.

Mary had come to Jerusalem for the Passover. Her hopes must have mounted on Palm Sunday. But hardly had the crowd dispersed when she began to hear whispers of impending doom. It was said that the temple authorities were planning to dispose of him. She had remained close by when he was arrested. She had shed tears during the trial, hoping against hope that a friendly voice would be raised in his defense. When he was condemned to die, she wanted to cry out in protest. She had walked close behind him on the long journey to the place of crucifixion.

Mary had no thought for herself as she waited for the end to come. She gave no consideration to what would happen to her when Jesus was gone. Her sister must have been concerned about it. The oldest son in the Jewish family was responsible for his parents' care. Where would Mary go after his death? Jesus thought about it too. Even while suffering the most intense pain, he noticed his mother standing close by the cross.

None of us can share the experience of Calvary without thinking seriously of our family relationships and asking ourselves whether we have met the obligations placed upon us to keep our home circle a part of the family of God.

Prayer

We give thee thanks this day, O Lord, for our home and family. Help us not to be so busy with other people that we have no time for those who are closest to us. May the spirit of Christ guide us to live well and nobly for those we love. In Jesus' name. Amen.

SECOND DAY

Companionship in Hours of Sorrow

Scripture: Read John 10:13-27

THERE WERE BITTER DISAPPOINTMENTS FOR JESUS THAT DAY ON Calvary. He had been forsaken by most of his followers. It must have meant a great deal to know that one of his disciples had overcome the natural fear of death to remain close by the cross.

John has been called "the beloved disciple." There are many reasons why he should have been given such an honor. By temperament he seems to have been lovable. He usually appears in marked contrast to the bombastic Peter. Though John and his brother James were referred to as the "sons of thunder," it is a different picture of John which we more often see. He caught the spirit of Christ before many of the others did. He may have been a son of thunder in the years before he met the Master, but he was changed when Jesus laid claim upon his loyalty.

John was with the Master during many of the intimate experiences of his public ministry. When a small group of disciples was selected to share a moment of spiritual significance, John was always one of them. Jesus wanted him close by because John understood his motives and aims better than some of the others. This beloved follower had qualities which made him responsive to Christ.

It is not a matter of chance that men who practice the teachings of Jesus with earnest devotion are those who come to be like him. Francis of Assisi set out to live according to the spirit of the Master and came to reflect many of his personal qualities.

Albert Schweitzer has endeavored to pattern his work after that of the man from Nazareth. It is significant that one who attended a luncheon in Schweitzer's honor in Chicago commented, "I have never before had such a feeling come over me. That man seemed more like Jesus than any man I have ever known."

We can understand why the Master turned to John when

he was concerned about his mother's future. No one in his circle of followers and friends was so well equipped to help him. Jesus looked into John's face. "Behold thy mother," he said.

It is probable that Jesus would have asked a younger brother to be responsible for his mother if the brother had been there. But John was chosen. He would be entrusted with many of Jesus' commands during the years ahead. It is understandable why Christ should give this very personal assignment to the one who followed him so earnestly and who loved him so deeply.

Concern for his mother's welfare, important as it must have been, was not the only factor in the situation. The Master must have known that his mother and his closest follower would find comfort in each other's company. The hours would not seem so endless if they could be together.

The bitterest sorrow is always easier to bear if it is shared with a friend or a loved one who understands. Many a father or mother would have broken under the strain which came from losing a child, but because they were together and had each other, they were able to bear the loss. John Gunther describes how he and his wife found each other and found meaning in suffering when their son lost the gallant fight with death. The Rev. Tanimoto, minister of the Methodist Church in Hiroshima, Japan, tells how mutual anguish enabled thousands of victims of atomic bombing to go on living. When weak and exhausted by sorrow, our strength is renewed if we can share our grief with someone who loves us.

All of us need the support of someone who understands and sympathizes. Often it is given by those within the family circle, but frequently the answer to the needs of our hearts is to be found in the Christian fellowship. Because the Church is the family of God, we can share our joys and sorrows with those who are our brothers and sisters in the faith.

Prayer

We thank thee, O God, that we never need to walk alone. Thy presence is with us each hour of the day in the silence of our own thoughts and in the touch of a human hand. Help us to share with others in need the joy which thou hast given to us. In Jesus' name. Amen.

THIRD DAY

Service in Hours of Sorrow

Scripture: Read Eph. 3:14-21

The thoughts of John during the hours of the crucifixion are not recorded in the Gospels. It is strange how quickly a man's mind turns toward future plans when he is certain that death is at hand. He looks ahead even while the tragedy is unfolding. That is one of God's blessings in time of sorrow. It was so when a group of civic leaders in Texas City, Texas, met to plan a new and more beautiful community even while flames were raging uncontrolled and life and property in their city were being destroyed.

It would have been natural for John to be looking ahead during the hours while he waited for death to come. He may have been planning revenge upon those who had plotted the death of his Master. Perhaps he was listing the names of those who deserved punishment because of their actions that day. Or he may have been thinking of his own future, saying,

"I'll go back to the fishing fleet on the Sea of Galilee to make a new start."

Jesus knew the danger which might result if plans for the future were formulated too quickly. His summons to "behold thy mother" became a challenge to immediate responsibility as a substitute for bitter thoughts. John couldn't bother with hate now; he had a woman to care for. He couldn't go back to the old life, not now; he had a work to complete for his Master. The words of Jesus kept him from thoughts and deeds which might have marred his life.

An hour of abject sorrow is never the time to make decisions which will affect a lifetime. Giuseppe Verdi renounced a musical career when he was refused admission to the conservatory in Rome. It was only by chance that the fruits of his genius were not lost to the ages because of that hasty resolution. Thomas Hardy at one time decided to give up writing as a career when his works were rejected by unsympathetic editors. If he had not been persuaded to reconsider his decision, the world of letters would have lost one of its most gifted figures. No one is wise who makes plans for a lifetime during a moment of tragedy.

Whatever John had contemplated as his future course of action must now be put aside while he took care of the mother of his Lord. Responsibility saved him from decisions which might have seriously impaired his power to further the Christian cause. Many of us will be spared unfortunate decisions in time of sorrow if we find work to do or loads to lift.

Peace treaties which were written during or immediately after the cruel experience of war have often seemed shameful documents when looked upon from the vantage point of later years. It was wiser for a nation to search out places of need and to help heal the ugly wounds which war had left, before resorting to punishment of the guilty. It was the best way for John, and it is best for people in the twentieth century.

Someone has said that the cross of Jesus became the crossroads of the world. All the qualities in human life which cause men to stoop to deeds of horror were found there. Humanity reached its lowest point that day. But that is not all! The grace of God and his mercy were revealed. We see here also a manifestation of the soul of man reaching new heights of love and devotion.

"Behold thy mother. . . . Behold thy son." The drama of human need and the answer which consecrated service makes to that need were dramatically pictured by the words of Christ from the cross. They will forever challenge us to consider the will of God when tragedy seems to have made life unbearable.

Prayer

Dear Lord, help us to do thy will in every moment of our lives. Save us from the doubts and despairs which so often threaten us. Help us to wait on thee, and in the waiting may we find the answer to our needs and strength to live nobly as followers of Jesus. In his name we pray. Amen.

FOURTH DAY

God Seen Through the Family

Scripture: Read Luke 15:11-32

THE WORDS OF JESUS ON THE CROSS DEAL IN CAPSULE FORM with the deepest problems of life. Forgiveness, salvation, human suffering, the relationship of God and man, and immortality—these are all of momentous importance. The Cross dramatizes our longing for certainty and, at the same time, provides the answer to our spiritual quest.

The family relationship was sacred to Christ. The faith which he proclaimed was dramatized in terms of the family more frequently than in any other way. Even the Cross has its contribution to make to this theme.

The religion of Jesus begins in the home. He gathered the scattered members of the human family together by saying, "When ye pray, say, Our Father." "Father" was the term which he used most frequently when he talked of God. The affectionate and intimate picture of the Eternal which this suggests has sometimes stirred resentment in those who are satisfied to keep God an awesome mystery, approachable only through the help of an intermediary. The Italian Venini was condemned to death for daring to speak of God as having the qualities and availability of an earthly father. When he was led out to the place of execution, he is reported to have stooped to pick up a blade of straw, saying: "Had I no other evidence for the fatherhood of God, this blade of straw would be enough for me."

Edwin Holt Hughes wrote:

The God and Father of Jesus Christ is the only foundation for the family life of humanity. Robbing the world of its real parent-hood, we shall turn it into an orphan asylum wherein a coercive institutionalism must take the place of the warm and vital elements of a genuine home.[1]

Jesus recognized God as his father. His parables remind us that God has a concern for men like the concern of a father for his children. He encouraged his followers to talk to God as to an earthly parent.

[1] *God's Family* (Nashville: Abingdon Press, 1926), pp. 132-33.

The home was basic in the teachings of Jesus about man's approach to God. Like the attitude of a son and daughter to their parents should be that of the worshiper to the great Jehovah. He dramatized the good will of the Creator by saying, "Like as a father pitieth his children, so the Lord . . . ." The encircling love of God was felt whenever men recognized and respected him. Jesus pictured the goal of human relationships as a world in which the principles of the family will govern every community, national, and international situation. He left no doubt of the fact that we are "children of God," and therefore all kindred.

There is a book titled *God's Stepchildren*. A Hottentot living in darkest Africa asks, "Are we brown people simply God's stepchildren?" Such an idea is unacceptable to an earnest follower of Jesus, to one who has become aware of the lofty spiritual possibilities of all people. We are children of God and therefore brothers. This truth is central in the revelation which came to the world in Christ.

The Cross has an eternal value for each one of us. Everlasting truth was revealed on Calvary. The emphasis in the Third Word, "Woman, behold thy son! . . . Behold thy mother!" makes the human family relationships sacred. It also gives us a picture of God's concern for all his children.

Prayer

Forgive us, O God, when we deny our family relationship with thee. It is easy for us to forget that thou art a Father and that all men are thy children. Purge us of all that is unworthy in our thoughts, and may our deeds give evidence of our willingness to be thy sons and daughters and brothers and sisters to all thy children. In Jesus' name. Amen.

FIFTH DAY

Self-Sacrifice as a Key to God's Nature

Scripture: Read Phil. 2:1-15

JOHN WAS ASSIGNED A DIFFICULT TASK WHEN JESUS SAID, "BE-
hold thy mother!" It would involve many years of loving service. He could never again regard his time and material goods
as his own. He had a mother to care for, and she was the
mother of his Master.

Sacrificial love is pictured here as an important part of the
Christian life. It suggests that casual devotion is not enough.
We have been entrusted with tasks and responsibilities which
demand our best.

Such consecration to a noble cause was, in small measure,
an example of the sacrifice which Jesus himself made. He
gave his strength without thought of comfort or ease. He
healed the sick and was unwearying in his labors in behalf of
those who were in need. And, at the last, his acceptance of
the Cross as the method to win men to him became an unmatched demonstration of love in action.

We often substitute some other approach for the way of
love. A willingness to accept suffering is frequently tossed aside
as a poor substitute for the use of material or physical power.

Nations seem to gain their ends by coercion. Parents often
believe strict commands are more effective than the love which
is patient and knows no end. But time provides evidence that

61

force is futile. The world needs the persuasion which is made possible by sacrifice.

Dostoevsky in *The Brothers Karamazov* relates the fable of the Grand Inquisitor. During the days of the Inquisition Jesus returned to earth and visited those who were persecuted. As he moved about the city, men forgot for a time their cares and their sorrows. He healed the sick as he did of old. He gave freely of himself to help others. Sacrifice was his way and his life.

The Grand Inquisitor ordered Christ arrested. That night he visited Jesus in his prison cell. The Inquisitor said:

I know why Thou art come. Thou art come to repeat thy great mistake in the wilderness, and to spoil our work. What did the great and wise Spirit offer Thee there? Just the three things by which men may be controlled: Bread, and Authority, and Mystery. But thou wouldest not; men were to follow Thee out of love and devotion, or not at all. We have had to correct Thy work or there would be few to follow Thee. And now Thou art come to repeat Thy great mistake and spoil our work; but it shall not be, for to-morrow I shall burn thee.[2]

Many of us are convinced that we know a better way than the one which Christ offered to his followers. Pride and greed and lust for power are still the instruments of our ambition. Sacrifice seems old-fashioned and outmoded when we are persuaded that we can more easily gain our desired ends by force.

While spoken to Mary, his mother, and to John, his beloved follower, the Third Word is an eternal reminder of the family relationship which binds us to God and to one another.

[2] (New York: E. P. Dutton & Co., 1927), p. 261.

It opens before us a way of life which demands a spirit of self-sacrifice like that of Christ.

Prayer

Dear Father, forgive us when we depend on money and influence to gain our desired ends. We have wandered far from the example which Jesus gave to his followers. Help us this day to test every word and deed by the measure of Christ. So shall we be thy disciples. In Jesus' name. *Amen.*

SIXTH DAY

Satisfying the Needs of Men

Scripture: Read Col. 3:1-25

LOVE WAS DEMANDED ON THE BASIS OF NEED IN THE THIRD WORD. Mary was lonely. During the months ahead she would be brokenhearted and afraid. She would need the love and support which came from the labor of someone who cared. Hers was a starkly clear need which no one could miss.

Within the human family there are longings which are never satisfied. In an exhibit of outstanding newspaper pictures one photograph captured continued interest from the spectators. It did not depict a devastating fire or a horrifying accident or a mass spectacle. It was a photograph of ordinary people on a busy street corner. Men and women from every walk of life were hurrying to places of business or pleasure. What arrested attention were the looks of worry and fear on the faces. No one seemed happy. The people reflected anxiety either with their own problems or with the problems of the world.

63

Anyone who lives close to people is aware of the acute problems which constantly must be faced. When we look beneath the surface of life, we find a heartbreak in unexpected places. Even those who seem completely to control their material and physical environments are carrying hidden burdens.

When confronted with the need of another person—whether friend or stranger—for material help and spiritual encouragement, it is easy to push aside the demand as someone else's responsibility. We tend quickly to avoid the issue by the assertion that the problem is not ours. Such an attitude is impossible when we live in the light of the Cross.

The Third Word of Jesus unites our interests with those whom we would call strangers or foreigners. Against our will we are drawn closer, as brothers and sisters, to one another. We are one family under the fatherhood of God.

No earnest seeker for truth can be deaf to the challenge of "behold thy mother." In that commission a responsibility is involved which must not be avoided while any mother or child or family is in need.

Hatred is no longer an acceptable quality of personality. The idea of the divine family stabs our conscience awake. It irritates our self-satisfactions. If we try to narrow our awareness of responsibility to include only our own community, or our own nation, or even our own hemisphere, we deny the message of the Cross.

Shakespeare's Shylock said that we are "fed with the same food, hurt with the same weapons." Christians recognize that people have qualities which they share in common. All have gifts from the God who is the Father of all of life.

Helen Keller's writings are full of gratitude for the contributions which others made to her development. She says: "I try to make the light in others' eyes my sun, the music in others' ears my symphony, the smile in others' lips my happiness." The followers of Jesus seek for the hidden values in those about them. Mary Slessor worked for twenty-nine years among the degraded and savage people of Calibar. The most feared tribes in all Africa were completely changed. She wrote in a letter to a friend: "My faith in Jesus helped me to see that color of skin and former ways of life are no barrier to keep men and women from becoming new creatures."

A steady gaze at the cross has always made a difference in the lives of those who waited there. The message of the crucified Christ belonged to his age, and it belongs to every age. It provides an unmatched reservoir of spiritual truth and power, but in return it demands our best in devoted service. It is often difficult to understand the full meaning of the fatherhood of God and the brotherhood of man, yet the acceptance of the divine family offers us a living hope for a better world.

Prayer

Help us, O Lord, to live in the light of the Cross. Our thoughts are too often shaped by the passing world about us. We are led into paths of action which are of men and not of thee. May the spirit of the Christ who was crucified give us strength to do thy will. In Jesus' name. Amen.

Solving the Riddle of Existence

Scripture: Read Mark 3:31-35

THE IDEA OF THE DIVINE FAMILY DOES SOMETHING to us in changing our attitudes and outlooks, but it also does something for us. Jesus answered many questions we all have asked when he spoke of God as a Father.

The fatherhood of God is not a strange doctrine to those who have studied the Gospels. The word "Father" is used only 7 times in the Old Testament to describe Jehovah, but in the New Testament it is used 227 times. The majority of the references are in the words of Jesus.

We go to the Cross to find an answer to many of our questions concerning the nature of God. Man has never received a clearer witness of the divine nature than when he climbed to the summit of Calvary.

The words of Jesus, "Mother, behold thy son! . . . Behold thy mother!" summon us to sympathy and service. We recognize a deepened responsibility to our loved ones because of the concern of Jesus for his mother. There is even more to be learned from these words. Christians stand breathless to catch each syllable which came from the lips of the Master. The Third Word gives us a pattern for the relationship between God and man which meets the stern test of every century.

John the Divine suggested many years later what that revelation meant to the early church. "Behold, what manner of love

he Father hath bestowed upon us, that we should be called
he sons of God," he wrote. Children of God and therefore
brothers and sisters! This was the legacy of the Cross to bewildered humanity. Even today it provides a solution to the
hatreds and misunderstandings which divide the people of
every nation.

Crowds are frequently attracted to what is known as a "Flea
Circus." Standing around a table, the onlookers watch minute
fleas cavorting like men. They drag tiny wagons; they tumble
and perform. People enjoy watching these carefully planned
imitations of some of the common activities in the life of man.
And you and I, are we not boastfully proud of our greatness
when we strut about on the human stage? Yet we are pilgrims
upon an earth which is so infinitesimally small that if our
largest telescopes were placed on another planet, our world
would appear as only a speck. And beyond the planets is an
immeasurable space in which the stars are as numerous as
sands of the sea.

Carved over the entrance to the Singing Tower in Florida
are the words:

> I come here to find myself,
> It's so easy to get lost in the world.

It is easy to become confused by the problems of our complex civilization. We often plead for an understanding of human existence. If we are to find an answer to the questions of
man's destiny, we need the guidance which is offered by the
Christian faith.

The vastness of the universe is brought within the focus of
our understanding by the words of Jesus from the cross. The
mystery of life is cleared. We claim here our place in the divine
family. God is forever the Father; we are forever his children.

Before the majesty of the scene we stand in hushed silence. We are aware that life has sublime meaning.

Prayer

Give us, O God, a vision of life as thou hast intended it to be. Lift our horizons so we may understand thy matchless love for each of us. Save us this day from the petty thoughts which would deny thy purposes for all mankind. Help us to know thee as Father and to live as thy children. In Jesus' name. Amen.

FOURTH WEEK

"My God, My God, Why Hast Thou Forsaken Me?"

—*Matt. 27:46*

FIRST DAY

When Suffering Brings Doubt

Scripture: Read Mark 15:24-38

ALL OF US UNDERSTAND THE CRY OF DESPAIR WHICH JESUS UT-
tered on the cross. Theologians may be embarrassed by a Christ
who sobbed out an admission of loneliness, but suffering men
and women in every age have been brought closer to God by
the realization that Jesus shared their misery and sorrow.

In every century we can peer into places where men have
died an untimely death and can hear their loved ones whisper,
"My God, my God, why hast thou forsaken me?" The cry
has come from the huts of peasants and from the castles of
kings; it has been heard alike in teeming cities and in jungle
outposts. In every age we can watch the collapse of human
dreams or the defeat of noble purposes and can listen to the
cry, "My God, my God, why . . . ?"

Booth Tarkington was informed by his physician that his
sight was fading, that he must assume he would be blind
within a year. His eyes had been strained by the steady pressure of many years of intense study. Darkness was closing
about him. "Where is there justice in the world, or providence
in a God who allows this kind of thing to happen?" he asked.

A tragic scene was enacted in a hospital in the state of New
Hampshire during an epidemic. The hospital was bulging
with those who were deathly sick. A man had been pacing
up and down the terrace, separated by a strict quarantine

from those who were dearer than life to him. For three days he had spent a large part of every hour in anxious waiting. Five members of his family had been brought to the hospital, victims of the plague. Four times he had been summoned to the office to receive the news that one of his loved ones was dead. Of the happy family of a week before only one of the sons remained. When a minister paused to offer words of comfort, the man turned upon him to voice an angry protest against God. But the anger quickly spent itself. "Why? Why?" the man kept asking. In his pitiful questioning we hear the sob of loneliness which is, at certain moments, the cry of all of us.

One day I followed a nurse down the corridor of an isolation hospital. We stopped by an iron lung in which a young bride of twenty-one was battling for her life. She had been stricken with paralysis only a few days before her soldier husband was expected to return home from foreign service. Every word was a struggle, but I could not fail to understand the gasping anguish when she asked, "Why did this happen to me?"

Unnumbered men and women have turned their eyes to the cross of Jesus when their faith has been stretched to the breaking point by pain or sorrow. Speculation concerning the meaning of their personal suffering may not have brought relief. But comfort and strength have come from the remembrance that they are not alone in the hour of trial. Jesus also bore his pain. He too felt a moment of abject loneliness. "Even Jesus?" they ask in awed wonder. It is true! Even Christ experienced a moment when he felt forsaken by his heavenly Father.

In the Louvre there is a picture which portrays Christ hanging on the cross. Nearby is the kneeling figure of a man who is evidently bearing a great sorrow. Under the cross is the inscription *"Et Maiora Sustinuit Ipse."* ("Greater pains than thine has he endured.")

The Fourth Word is a reminder to all of us that suffering is not a solitary and unique experience. It tells us that Christ felt the searing agony of continued pain.

Prayer

Dear Father, the miracle of thy concern for thy children is beyond our understanding. We can but worship and praise thy holy name. Help us this day to know that thou art near. May thy presence give us comfort in pain and courage to do thy will. In Jesus' name. Amen.

SECOND DAY

Beyond Doubt to Faith

Scripture: Read Matt. 26:36-46

SICKNESS OR DEATH OFTEN CAUSES US TO FERRET OUT PERSONAL failures or mistakes to justify the feeling that we have been forsaken by God. When tornadoes and floods devastated large areas in the wheat region of the United States, the victims of the tragedy probed for personal or social sins to explain what seemed an evidence of divine displeasure.

It is hard enough to bear suffering or sorrow without the added load of undeserved guilt. Much of the evil in the world is not caused by the mistakes of the individuals who suffer. The distress caused by war often falls upon those who had no part in the processes which led inevitably to the hour of

73

conflict. The scourge of disease creeps with relentless steps into the homes of those who are living by the laws of God.

The cry of loneliness from the lips of Jesus offers consolation. It is no longer necessary to resort to hidden sin to explain suffering, for Jesus suffered, and he was one who lived an exalted and blameless life. Why should we be oppressed by guilt because God seems for a time not to answer our prayers? Jesus felt forsaken in spite of the fact that he was closer to the heavenly Father than any other person who ever lived.

Though we are grateful for this word from the cross which reveals Jesus' human struggle in an hour of suffering, we must keep in mind that this cry was not his final one. It is encouraging in our times of weakness to know that the Master felt he was alone, but we can be glad this was not the only word which he uttered on Calvary.

There is no disgrace because we experience moments of doubt. One who has heretofore been firm in his faith should not rebuke himself because God at times seems far away. The doubter must finally march out beyond his misgivings to take his stand upon a solid foundation of trust. Doubt should never be more than a battleground where the struggle is carried on which ends with assurance and faith.

Bishop Hugh Latimer, of England, at one time questioned the goodness of God. When put to the test, he renounced his faith to escape the hardships of persecution. But Hugh Latimer's fame does not rest upon what he did in a moment of weakness. He is remembered because he came to an hour of courageous victory.

Helen Keller was deaf and blind and dumb. As a child she would lie on the ground, rolling and screaming in protest against a world which she could neither see nor hear. But

Helen Keller is not remembered because of her infirmities. Others have suffered handicaps and have been forgotten. She is remembered because she was able to accept divine help to push back the narrow walls in which she was confined.

It is never a mark of failure to doubt. Jesus experienced a few moments when it appeared that divine forces had conspired with human cruelty to blot out every hope. He felt that he had been forsaken by the Father whom he knew so well. In the hour of greatest agony he was tempted to doubt that God was there or that God was grieved by what was happening on Calvary.

Every man will wonder at times whether God is good. Do not rebuke him for it! Help him to walk out of the shadows of uncertainty into the light of faith. The cry of loneliness is not the final word from the cross! Nor should it be the final cry of any of us who are engulfed by sorrow.

Prayer

Forgive us for our doubts, O Lord. We often lose sight of thy presence in the problems which face us. Give us strength this day to trust thee in all things and to live according to thy purposes in every place we go. In Jesus' name. Amen.

THIRD DAY

The Compensations of Pain

Scripture: Read Matt. 11:25-30

FROM THE VANTAGE POINT OF HISTORY WE ARE ABLE TO SEE that values were realized on Calvary which outweighed the anguish. Jesus was certain of that during most of the tragic hours of suffering. Perhaps the intense pain blinded him for an instant to the miracle which was in the making. For a time nothing seemed real except the agony which he was bearing.

Some suffering brings little reward. At least no values are visible at the time. But much human pain has its compensations. It leaves strange residues in changed lives and nobler outlooks.

E. Stanton Turner was the general secretary of the Y.M.C.A. in the Philippines when war broke out in the Orient. He spent three difficult years in a concentration camp. He dwells at length upon the values which came to him during that period. He lost a great deal, but he gained even more. He likens his experience and those of his fellow sufferers to the hardships of the early disciples. "The Disciples needed the Cross to awaken them to truths which they had taken for granted," he says. "Without the Cross there could have been no Church."

The disciples needed the Cross! They grew in grace and spiritual strength through suffering. Many of us discover a richer and fuller life as a result of pain. Our values are reborn; our faith is rekindled. Friendships are deepened; divided families are brought together. Suffering is an instrument which is like a surgeon's knife! It cuts and it scars, but it makes possible the hope of a better life.

Charles Y. Harrison was stricken with a heart attack. At first the illness seemed an unmitigated tragedy. The weeks of continued pain in the hospital were followed by months of slow recuperation. His physician laid down strict rules which seemed the end of all normal living. Yet after a year of convalescence he wrote a book titled *Thank God for My Heart Attack*. He described some of the values which resulted from the suffering. He says:

You've been given a second chance in a world where millions are given not even a first chance. You feel like a condemned man who has been saved by a last-minute reprieve. Life, henceforth, will never be something to be taken for granted or to spend with prodigality . . . . Something happens to your way of looking at things after a heart attack. Your eye is no longer jaded or sharply critical, and sees subtle nuances in everything.[1]

It is often difficult to find the light which streams through pain. But suffering should never be tested at a time when pain is at its worst. Nor can God's presence or absence from the place of anguish be determined by the suffering which is involved. Eternal purposes often mold hope and victory out of a texture of hardship.

Suffering offers us an opportunity to demonstrate the vitality of our faith. It is our duty and privilege to remain true to God in times of adversity. C. S. Lewis in *The Screwtape Letters* has the devil say:

Our cause is never more in danger than when a human, no longer desiring, but still intending, to do our Enemy's [i.e., God's] will, looks around upon a universe from which every trace of Him seems to have vanished, and asks why he has been forsaken, *and still obeys*.[2] [Italics mine.]

We can understand why Jesus spoke the word of loneliness. It is a cry which resounds across the centuries in a recurring echo. Forsaken! Forsaken by God!

Questioning doubt was not the final note sounded by Jesus. Only a few moments were to pass before he gave evidence of perfect trust in God's providential care. He spoke then with confident assurance. His faith and trust will always be an ex-

[1] (New York: Henry Holt & Co., 1949), pp. 2-3.
[2] (New York: The Macmillan Co., 1943), p. 47.

ample of the finest response which any of us can give to the problem of suffering.

Prayer

Help us this day, O Lord, to see the light that shines through pain. Give us the courage to look beyond the burdens and defeats which may confront us to the hope which tomorrow may bring. In all things help us to know thee and to trust in thy everlasting care for each one of us. In Jesus' name. Amen.

FOURTH DAY

God as Seen in Christ

Scripture: Read Rom. 8:24-39

GOD WAS IN CHRIST! THAT IS THE CENTRAL FACT IN THE CHRIStian gospel. The teachings of Jesus during his public ministry reveal the eternal truth. The transcendent nature of that revelation is evident in the Crucifixion. God was at work in Christ during the long hours when he hung in helpless agony.

An impressive picture of Calvary can be seen in the National Gallery in London. Christ is on the cross, almost hidden in the darkness. At first the one who looks observes nothing but the blackness and through it the dim figure of the suffering Christ. But if his gaze does not falter, he glimpses a figure with arms outstretched, tenderly holding up the suffering one. His face is twisted by a pain which is more agonizing even than that of the Christ. God the Father is grieving with his Son as he hangs on the cross.

When the Words spoken by Jesus on Calvary are examined

78

in the light of the fact that God was revealing his nature by the events which occurred that day, they assume a significance which is timeless. It is possible to analyze and weigh them with a view to finding a key to the heart and mind of God. A panorama of eternal significance unfolds before the eyes of those who long to know the truth.

The Fourth Word came out of the abject misery of continued pain. "My God, my God, why hast thou forsaken me?" cried the Christ.

At first these words seem completely human. They appear to be a desperate question which was born out of unrelieved agony. Many scholars have been satisfied to let them remain an evidence that even Christ experienced a moment when the face of his Father was blotted out.

It is reasonable to accept such an interpretation when we are searching for an answer to human pain in the words of Jesus. A cry of loneliness is understandable even when it comes from the lips of the most courageous of men.

Eternal truth was revealed on Calvary. The words of Jesus have a divine as well as a human message for humanity. What, then, can we learn from the Fourth Word?

Remember that God was in Christ, bearing all the agony accompanying the most cruel form of death known to man. God was feeling the pain. God in Christ was speaking words which were fraught with eternal meaning. Already he had declared that forgiveness is an attribute of the divine nature, already he had opened the portals of heaven for repentant souls in every generation, and he had lifted the family to an exalted place in the divine plan. When he uttered the Fourth Word, he was revealing another truth of everlasting significance.

The form of expression is less important than the truth it suggests. "My God, my God, why hast thou forsaken me?"

The question is from the first verse of the twenty-second psalm, a familiar passage to every faithful servant of Jehovah. It originally represented the pitiful cry of people who were oppressed by a conqueror. The tyrant had destroyed their holy places and had carried away the flower of their youth into slavery.

The heart of the cry is loneliness. It was prompted by suffering and heartbreak. When God in Christ used these words, he was revealing something about the divine nature which man has seldom understood. It tells us that God suffers! It reminds us that God is sometimes lonely! It announces that God's heart is often broken!

Prayer

We give thanks unto thee, O God, for thy witness in Christ. Our disappointments and despair have sometimes seemed too great to bear until we have remembered the Cross. Forgive us for our weaknesses. Give us strength to bear what life may bring each of us. In the suffering of Jesus may we find courage to be faithful to thee. In Jesus' name. Amen.

FIFTH DAY

Man's Sin Is God's Burden

Scripture: Read II Cor. 4:1-18

THE ANCIENT GREEKS BOASTED OF GODS WHO MOVED FROM AGE to age undisturbed by earthly troubles; no cry of suffering humanity pierced their protective shells; their lives were an endless procession of untroubled days. That is not the God who was revealed on Calvary. The Father who was seen in Jesus cares for the world and suffers because of its sin.

In the Old Testament, Jehovah is often pictured as a harsh deity whose interest in humanity is limited to occasions when men have transgressed his laws. Slowly the Hebrew people came to realize that Jehovah is a loving, even a suffering God. Isaiah declares that "in all their affliction he was afflicted." The prophet Hosea gave his listeners a clear portrait of the God who claimed man's allegiance, who was a God of mercy, suffering because of the sins of his people.

The portrait of God which is suggested by the Fourth Word is not a solitary view. It is assumed in a number of passages in the Old Testament. It is central in all of the teachings of Jesus. Here on the cross the revelation moves out of the area of discussion and speculation. It is dramatically clear that God suffers! You may turn your eyes away if you like. Some earnest seekers do not want to look upon a God who was borne down by grief; they wish they could avoid gazing upon what they think is a humiliation of the divine Creator. But as we look at the cross, we see more than that! The nature of God stands out in stark realism.

There is a reason for the suffering of the heavenly Father. His wisdom is greater than man's wisdom, and his love is deeper than man's love. God is therefore grieved by the failures of his children. In the process of creation he had matched man's possibilities with the fullness of the world. He had placed at the disposal of man all he required to live as a child of God. The heavenly Father knew each step of the way when man failed to accept the challenge of his opportunity. He was aware of the times when his children missed the upward road. Because man could be so noble and yet was so depraved, God was troubled. "Thou hast made him [man] a little lower than the angels, and hast crowned him with glory and honour," declared the psalmist. Human beings were made in the "image of God," endowed with high and holy possibilities. The knowledge that the gulf between himself and humanity —which in the beginning was so narrow—was growing continually wider as man sought satisfactions of a purely material nature made God feel lonely. He suffered because of man's mistakes.

It is humbling and disturbing to remember that God continues to suffer when we fail to obey his laws. The words of Jesus remind us that we have the power to break the heart of the Eternal.

Prayer

Forgive us, O God, for those thoughts and deeds which bring thee sorrow. We have hated when we ought to have loved. We have criticized when we ought to have praised. We have thought of self when we ought to have thought of others. Our lives are too often a denial of our faith. Give us strength this day to do thy will. In Jesus' name. Amen.

SIXTH DAY

God's Limitation in Human Freedom

Scripture: Read II Cor. 12:1-11

GOD MUST HAVE BEEN TEMPTED TO DESTROY HUMAN FREEDOM when men continued to break his commandments. He could have swept aside sin in an instant. He could have made an eternal Garden of Eden out of the ruins brought about by human greed and selfishness.

In his infinite wisdom God knew that such a plan would destroy the reason for the creation. To withdraw the right of choice would relegate man to the role of puppet. He might become a strong man and healthy specimen of God's creating genius, but he would remain forever a mere figure moved about at the whim of his Maker.

A newborn baby is unable to make decisions. Except by the exercise of tiny lungs it is helpless to influence the pattern of its life. But as the child grows in stature, a wise parent helps him to think through the situations which require a choice. If the parent continues to direct the life of his child and deprives him of the right of decision, a tragedy is in the making. A life which is sheltered often ends in unhappiness. Soonor or later a growing child wants a part in shaping his way of life. If he is not given that opportunity, he either becomes a person of flabby, insipid moral fiber, or he breaks the bonds which bind him.

God did not take away the freedom which he had entrusted to man, even when it seemed that his children were bent on destroying themselves. He was patient when man turned away from the privilege of close fellowship with him.

Human freedom is not the only factor which keeps God from interfering with us when we choose evil ways. He has placed his confidence in the natural processes of the universe. The abiding laws of nature prevent him from standing between us and the consequences of our deeds.

In many parts of the United States vast areas of woodland have been stripped of every tree in order to provide lumber for the markets of the world. Stumps dot the waste areas, a ghostly reminder of the beauty which once covered those mountainsides. The stripping of the hills enabled certain individuals to gain the material satisfactions which they craved.

But now the descendants of those who destroyed the woods are victimized by floods which sweep down the naked mountain slopes to become raging streams.

Remember that God in his wisdom knows the disaster which will result from a lack of concern for the forests. Yet he is helpless to do more than impart warning of the disaster. When the floods come and homes are swept away, he suffers with humanity. He offers comfort to those who maintain fellowship with him. But it is not his will to abrogate the natural laws which he has established.

When we stop to think about it, we would not want God to interfere with his laws. We would be continually bewildered if we could not trust the universe to be orderly. So God must suffer when greed brings stark tragedy to the world.

God experienced a moment of utter loneliness when human arrogance and hatred sent Christ to the cross. The words of the man of Galilee revealed the depth of anguish in the heart of the Creator.

Prayer

When we look at the cross of Jesus, O Lord, the evil in our lives makes us ashamed. Our boasting of virtue has a hollow sound. Our selfishness has brought thee sorrow. Even if we had a lifetime to make amends, it would not be enough. Help us to use what time we have to do thy will. Help us to use all thy gifts for thy glory. In Jesus' name. Amen.

SEVENTH DAY

The Price of Evil to God

Scripture: Read I Thess. 3:1-13

WE ASSUME THAT THE HEAVENLY FATHER IS INDIGNANT WHEN we fail to keep his laws or when we refuse to allow his spirit to guide us. That is understandable. But look to the cross if you want to learn how God is affected by our shortcomings, how he is wounded by our mistakes.

God's grief is caused by human failure. When we deny him in our willful desire to follow the way of the world, he is sorrowful. When we curse his name, or when we speak up before others to express doubts concerning his justice, he does not turn away from us. When we take part in plans and share in social customs which postpone his ultimate triumph in the world, he does not rage against us. In such moments he feels forsaken and lonely.

The criminal class in society did not condemn Jesus to death. The thieves, the murderers, and the convicts had no quarrel with him. The most respectable people in Jerusalem killed him—men who were guilty of religious narrowness, of political ambition, and of financial self-interest. God suffered because of the sins which, even today, are surrounded by an atmosphere of respectability.

Religious bigotry still divides people into many groups. Some prattle of their holiness while every day they undermine the teachings of Christ by their betrayal of the truth which

85

he came to reveal. Political ambition still leads men into courses of action in which honor and the opportunity to serve others seem less significant than the material gain which is involved. Financial self-interest still shapes attitudes and prompts actions which are foreign to the Christian message.

The God whose nature was revealed in Christ continues to suffer in our day. He is bruised by every blow which is inflicted by our selfishness or greed.

That is the message of the Fourth Word. Sin, neglect, hatred—all of these cause God to suffer. The Cross reveals the pain which God felt when he was misunderstood and denied. He will continue to be bruised and hurt and crucified until the day when man turns his face toward the light.

The universe is a single unit. All its parts belong together. The natural world and the world of men cannot be separated. Each of us has power either to defeat or to support the purposes of God by the way we live each day.

God needs us—each one of us—to abide by his laws of love. Our failure to do his will continues to give him grief.

Prayer

O God, we are humbled by the reminder that thou dost need us to accomplish thy purposes for the world. Forgive us for the many times this day when our thoughts and our deeds may give thee sorrow. Help us to do thy will in all we endeavor to accomplish. In the name of Jesus. Amen.

FIFTH WEEK

"I Thirst."

—*John 19:28*

FIRST DAY

Jesus Speaks for the Needy
Scripture: Read John 19:23-29

THE TRAGEDY ON CALVARY WAS NEAR AN END. THE HEAT OF THE day and the closeness of death had taken the sharp edge of enthusiasm from those who were using the occasion to heap a final ridicule upon Christ. The crowd was silent.

The parched lips of the Master moved. Speech was difficult. "I thirst!" he whispered.

We understand such a cry! There have been times when we too have been hot and thirsty. We have wanted a cool drink after a period of physical testing which could not be compared to that which Jesus experienced.

The Master was pleading for a friendly hand to perform a desperately needed service. It was a soldier, evidently, who responded. A vessel of vinegar had been brought from the city. He dipped a sponge into the dish, set the sponge on a stick, and lifted it to the mouth of Jesus. For whatever it was worth, that kindness was extended to him. His lips at least were moistened.

Christians have weighed each of the seven recorded utterances of Jesus from the cross. Keys to eternal truth have been suggested by the words which he spoke. The obvious physical need of the Master which brought forth the Fifth Word has often led students of the Gospels to dispose of it as merely an added clue to the depth of suffering which he endured.

But the Cross gives hints of spiritual certainty which help to satisfy the needs of men in every generation. It etches the longings and hopes of all mankind, as well as the faith by which each of us may live. That is the mission of the Fifth Word. "I thirst!" is a dramatic picture of something real, something tragic, which is always happening in the world.

Francis of Assisi came to an hour when the events which occurred on Calvary were the supreme concern of his life. He listened intently to the words which were spoken by the Christ. From then on he began to hear a sad, lonely murmur of need in every street and byway. "I thirst!" came from the lips of little children who were hungry and homeless. "I thirst!" came from the outcasts and the unwanted in a hundred Italian villages. The voice of Jesus asking for something to drink was a summons to Francis to quicken his hearing to the endless cries of people for help.

Before he understood what the Cross demanded of him, Francis had passed by beggars and cripples without giving them a second glance. He enjoyed the pleasures of daily living too much to be aware of its tragedy. That attitude was changed when he recaptured the events of the first Good Friday. A steady gaze at the crucified Christ transformed his manner of living. As he walked the busy streets or loitered in the noisy market place, he heard the cry of pitiful men and women and children on every hand.

Unless we are satisfied to allow the Cross to remain merely a pageant, the same experience will be repeated in our daily lives. When we think only of ourselves, the suffering of Jesus remains a drama which has no meaning. It never pierces the armor which we carry to protect privilege and possessions against Christ's insistent demand that every attitude and outlook be refined. Those of us who are determined to make Jesus the Lord and Master of our lives will test all we say and all we do by the Cross. We will hear Jesus' cry "I thirst" in every pitiful entreaty which comes from needy humanity.

Prayer

Dear Father, we thank thee for the eternal truth which shines through Calvary. Help us to hear this day the cry of Christ wherever there is human need. Forgive us for our blindness to the sufferings of people and our deafness to the calls of help which come from far and near. Use us as those who are willing to do thy will. We pray in the name of Jesus. Amen.

SECOND DAY

The Cross Makes Life Different

Scripture: Read Matt. 25:14-30

While commanding a ship engaged in slave trade in South Atlantic waters, Sir John Newton wrote the words of a familiar hymn:

> Amazing grace! how sweet the sound,
>   That saved a wretch like me!
> I once was lost, but now am found,
>   Was blind, but now I see.

As Sir John labored to finish that verse, a wail could be heard from the lips of hundreds of men imprisoned in the foul hold of his ship. But he did not hear. He declared: "I was blind, but now I see." What he saw was a cross which did something for him without doing anything to him. He could talk glibly about the beauty of the Crucifixion without sensing any of the agony which was involved.

Every part of the drama which unfolded on Calvary has a vital message for ears that are sensitive. We will be forever different because of what occurred that day. It is impossible to hear Jesus cry, "I thirst!" and then go back to a narrow and blind outlook on life. The suffering of Jesus typifies the suffering which marks the lot of millions of people throughout the world. When we listen to his words, we must hear also the cries of needy men.

The plea for help continues in our day in the voices of countless hungry and dispossessed people of many nations. Sensitive spirits in every generation have heard the cry, for the starving have always been with us. But the number of the needy is more numerous now than ever before. Writing about the peoples of the Orient, John Gunther declared that millions of men and women are born, live, and die without knowing what it means to have a full stomach. Always hungry! And sometimes confronting periods of famine when death claims a host of people because there is no bread to eat.

The political condition of the world has added to the pressure of want. "I thirst!" is the cry of thousands of orphans and widows who are victims of long years of conflict in Europe and Asia. Christ's plea has been repeated millions of times in this generation by those who have learned what it means to lose all they possess except the will to live.

It is difficult to stand in silent adoration at the foot of the cross without having our attitudes toward people changed. The plea of Jesus for physical help must, if it means anything at all, be translated into the call of suffering men in our streets.

Georgia Harkness expresses this irresistible pull of the cross when she says:

> I listen to the agony of God—
>> I who am fed,
>> Who never yet went hungry for a day.
>> I see the dead—
>> The children starved for lack of bread—
>> I see, and try to pray.
>
> I listen to the agony of God—
>> I who am warm,
>> Who never yet have lacked a sheltering home.
>> In dull alarm
>> The dispossessed of hut and farm
>> Aimless and "transient" roam.
>
> I listen to the agony of God—
>> I who am strong,
>> With health, and love, and laughter in my soul.
>> I see a throng
>> Of stunted children reared in wrong,
>> And wish to make them whole.
>
> I listen to the agony of God—
>> But know full well
>> That not until I share their bitter cry—
>> Earth's pain and hell—
>> Can God within my spirit dwell
>> To bring His kingdom nigh.[1]

[1] "The Agony of God," *The Glory of God* (Nashville: Abingdon Press, 1943), p. 16. Used by permission.

Jesus is speaking again. His words have a message for all of us. "I thirst!" he whispers. If we are willing to listen, we hear in his words the plea of a hungry and suffering world.

Prayer

Hear our prayer, O Lord, for the hungry and dispossessed people of the earth. Make us thy servants to use what we have to help lift their burden of suffering. Stir us to awareness lest we be self-satisfied. May the Spirit of the crucified Christ claim our loyalty, our love, and our service. In his name we pray. Amen.

THIRD DAY

Meeting the Spiritual Needs of Men
Scripture: Read Matt. 25:31-46

HUMAN NEED IS NO LESS URGENT WHEN THE CRY IS FOR SOME-thing more than water and bread. Other unsatisfied longings cripple the daily lives of people. The suffering of the world is not limited to that which can be satisfied by material goods alone.

Egas Moniz, a Portuguese surgeon, has built an international reputation by the development of what is known as psychic surgery. He has succeeded in blocking off certain portions of the brain of patients who are victimized by excessive worry or anxiety. It is claimed that many have found relief through his operation.

Whatever may be the permanent values of Dr. Moniz' experiments, they dramatize the fact that a large segment of the human family is suffering from the need for something more than food or drink. To resort to a surgeon's knife to cure fear and worry is a poor kind of substitute for a healing power which comes from sympathy and understanding and from the practical aid of applied Christianity. When victims of fear beg for spiritual help, it is inevitable that those who claim Jesus as their Lord and Master should want to offer their assistance.

Mrs. Glenn Frank suffered an almost insuperable blow when her brilliant husband and her only son were killed in an automobile accident. She lived through weeks of anguish when she was plagued by the thought that there was no reason why she should continue to live. She longed to escape from the empty world in which she seemed merely to be existing. Then one day a mother came to see her who had recently lost a son. "I didn't want to live," the woman said to Mrs. Frank. "Then a friend who had known you and your husband and son told me about you. You lived. Yet I who had a son and daughter and a husband left wanted to die." The woman helped Mrs. Frank to find a reason to go on living. It was her mission to give encouragement to hundreds of those who through sorrow had come to feel that their world had collapsed.

That kind of response always occurs when an earnest seeker makes a pilgrimage to the cross. To hear the cry of Jesus for physical aid solicits from us the best we have to help his followers in every part of the world.

It is customary in this generation for those with a critical approach to religion to cite the failures of Christianity. They delight in pointing out the places where our Christian civilization is at variance with the teachings of the Master. Yet, for better or worse, the fate of the world depends upon our ability to transform the teachings of Christ into individual and social behavior. Scorn is not needed so much as penitence and consecration.

Nicolas Berdyaev declared:

A new Christian piety must be revealed in our world. And upon this new Christian piety depends the fate of the world and that of man. It cannot be an abstract form, retirement from the world and from mankind: it must be a form of spiritual effort exerted over man and his world.[2]

The longings of humanity are numerous. "I thirst!" is an oft-repeated cry. The need for food and drink, for friendship and security, take their toll of human strength. When we have once watched with those on Calvary, we will never be satisfied to live selfishly. We will hear the plea of Jesus whenever we look into the sad eyes of those who are suffering.

Prayer

Help us to tread softly today, O God, listening for the cries of need wherever they may be. Give us alert minds and sympathetic hearts. Enable us to be the representatives of Christ within the walls of our homes and in the place where we work. Receive now the dedication which we make of ourselves that in all things we may be the disciples of Christ. In his name we pray. Amen.

[2] *The Fate of Man in the Modern World*, Donald A. Lowrie (New York: Morehouse-Gorham Co., 1935), p. 117.

FOURTH DAY

Satisfying the Thirst of the Soul
Scripture: Read Matt. 17:21-27

MEN EXPERIENCE MANY KINDS OF THIRST. A TRAVELER WHO walks a long and dusty road under the blistering rays of a summer sun is thirsty for a cool drink of water. On the other hand, men speak of a thirst for understanding and sympathy. It is said that during his boyhood Abraham Lincoln had a thirst for knowledge. The meaning of the word "thirst" has been broadened to include many basic desires which cannot be satisfied by a quantity of liquid so much as by a quality of life.

The Fifth Word is a plea for water. The mounting pain which Jesus felt as he hung on the scorching summit of Calvary's scarred hill leaves no room to doubt that his plea was for water. His dry and cracked lips spoke aloud of a mounting desire for something to drink.

But water was not all for which he thirsted. His cry was for more than could be satisfied by a liquid. That was evident when he turned his head away from the sponge, dripping with vinegar, which was lifted to his lips.

In the references which Jesus made to thirst during his public ministry the meaning is only once limited to a physical condition. That exception is in a parable in the twenty-fifth chapter of Matthew. In every other instance he taught his followers that man's thirst is to be quenched by satisfying the needs of the spirit.

97

The major emphasis in Jesus' ministry had been upon the soul of man. He pictured the world as a battleground in which the body and the spirit, the physical and the spiritual natures, are in a never-ending struggle. He yearned for a company of followers who would make wise choices between the temporal and the eternal, between the worldly and the heavenly. He said, "It is the spirit that quickeneth; the flesh profiteth nothing: the words that I speak unto you, they are spirit, and they are life." He continually minimized the importance of physical existence. "Fear not them which kill the body, but are not able to kill the soul," he said. He willingly accepted the agony of the Cross as a necessary means by which his followers might understand that the fate of the physical body is unimportant when compared to the significance of the soul.

The thirst of Jesus was for much more than water. His was the heart-rending cry of one who was putting forth his all for the world. He was seeking to call his followers from absorption in things. He was thirsting for understanding, for love, for a sign that some of us had glimpsed the meaning of his sacrifice.

The Gospels tell little of the plans which were made to care for the physical needs of Jesus during his public ministry. We learn that he was weary at times, but there is no indication that he was concerned for food or for drink or for shelter. That does not mean that he did not experience the normal demands of the body.

Christ's high hopes were in the realm of the spirit. He said those men were happy who "hunger and thirst after righteousness." His own hunger and thirst were satisfied whenever his disciples understood his message and mission. When Peter cried, "Thou art the Christ, the Son of the living God," Jesus' thirst was quenched. The consecrated devotion of those whom he loves still constitutes his meat and his drink.

Prayer

Dear God, forgive us if we have been with those on Calvary who merely watched Christ die. Help us to answer his needs by answering the needs of thy children wherever they may be. Enable us to transform our gratitude for the Cross into lives of sacrificial service. We make our prayer in the name of the crucified Christ. Amen.

FIFTH DAY

God Needs Our Faithfulness

Scripture: Read Rom. 12:1-21

THE MESSAGE OF CALVARY CROSSES ALL BARRIERS OF TIME AND space. The plea of Jesus to assuage his thirst is a recurring plea. It could not be satisfied once and for all that day in ancient Palestine. It echoes and re-echoes down to the end of time.

Jesus—as the Son of God—still thirsts for the devotion of his followers. Rejected and maligned by the world, he still longs for evidence that we have understood his work.

We are confronted in our day by major problems of existence. We face overpopulation, raising the question of whether the earth can cope with the increasing number of people who must have food and shelter. We are confronted by the danger that all life may be destroyed by the weapons which man has invented. No less important than these is the question of

99

whether we will become so completely absorbed in bodily satisfactions and material concerns that we will forget God.

Developments in our mode of life which give added comfort and security are in keeping with the will of the heavenly Father. Yet it is not in the divine plan that material security should be the final aim in life. With no higher goal to control our actions we become selfish. We struggle and fight to keep or to extend the number of our bodily satisfactions. Because we neglect the side of our nature which is eternal, we feel dissatisfied. Then we easily are victimized by anxiety and fear.

Jean Cocteau, the French philosopher, once visited the United States. He wrote upon his return to France:

New York is not a city that sits down. It is not a town that sleeps. . . . I am talking about a town that stands up because if it sat down it would rest, and it would think, and if it went to bed it would fall asleep and dream, and it wants neither to think nor to dream. . . . It wants to remain standing up, to forget, forget itself, wear itself out, and to escape by fatigue.[3]

This picture is disturbing because it describes many other cities. Millions of people are afraid to face their problems and even more afraid to confront the deeper questions of time and eternity.

It is inevitable that Christians should be infected by the germs of worldliness. The disease is widespread. Worldly satisfaction becomes a pleasant form of intoxication which enables us to forget for a time the graver responsibilities of life.

Maurice Maeterlinck pictured God sitting on a sunny mountain, smiling at the gravest offenses of men, regarding them as the naughtiness of puppies playing on the grass beneath him. Many of us who are revolted by such an idea are

[3] *Time*, June 13, 1949, p. 36.

living as if we believed it were true. We devote our strength and interest to material satisfactions. We do our work or pursue our pleasures believing either that God's back is turned so he does not see us or that he doesn't care what we do.

But God does care! The Cross is the supreme evidence of his concern. When Jesus uttered the Fifth Word, he voiced the eternal longing of the Father for the loyalty of his children. The cry cannot be satisfied by water. The God whom Christ reveals is thirsting for men and women who will help build his kingdom. He pleads for followers who will be true to his purposes. His thirst is quenched and his victory is made secure when we are faithful to his cause.

Prayer

Dear Father of us all, the world is too much with us. It has made us creatures in pursuit of material satisfactions rather than souls in quest of eternal life. Forgive us for our weaknesses. Help us to do thy will this day. Enable us to keep eternity in our hearts even as we struggle to bear the responsibilities which are ours. May the Cross hold us fast to the doing of thy will. In Jesus' name. Amen.

SIXTH DAY

Jesus Pleads for Loyalty to His Cause

Scripture: Read John 13:1-17

THE PHYSICAL NEEDS OF JESUS, AS WELL AS HIS SPIRITUAL LONGings, were satisfied when his followers showed courageous devotion to his cause. The seventy returned telling of the enthusiastic welcome which they had received. That news was better than a feast. The ready response of the twelve men who left their occupations to follow him gave Jesus the encouragement which enabled him to carry on his ministry of healing and teaching. His unfailing strength sprang from human as well as divine support.

It is doubtful whether Jesus would have said, "I thirst," if he had been able to look into the faces of the disciples. If Peter had cried out above the voices of the crowd, "Master, we are with thee!" if Thomas had been close enough to shout during a lull in the raucous laughter, "We have no doubt that thou wilt win the victory!" if Philip had spoken up to say, "My Master and my God!" it would have been different. But Jesus was alone! He was giving his all for humanity. Pain and scorn were his reward.

Jesus still thirsts for courageous and loyal devotion to his kingdom. He never promised that we would find it easy to follow him. He bluntly told his disciples that they would be denied many of the comforts of the world. When he appealed for their heroic devotion, he said that those who responded would be homeless and destitute.

Giuseppe Garibaldi is remembered as the patriot who saved the Roman republic, even though it appeared to die during his lifetime. The little state which had been founded on the site of the ancient city of Rome was under assault from the corrupt communities around it. The siege continued unabated for many weeks. Starvation and death were on every hand. When it appeared that surrender was inevitable, Garibaldi spoke to the assembled people. His faith and heroism had sustained the city again and again. "I am marching out of Rome today," he declared. "I offer neither quarters, nor provisions, nor wages; I offer hunger, thirst, forced marches, battles, death. Let him who loves his country with his heart and not with his lips only, follow me." The bravest of the men streamed after him into the hills to become the founders of the Italy of today. Garibaldi's appeal is strangely like the one which came from the lips of Jesus. "If any man will come after me," he said, "let him deny himself, and take up his cross daily, and follow me."

Thomas à Kempis said that if we wish the cross of Jesus to grip and hold our lives, we will accomplish that end not by arguing about what it means but by taking up his cross and following after him.

Jesus was aware of the perils which threatened the spread of the Kingdom. The dangers were partially caused by the hostility of the Roman soldiers, the Jewish authorities, and the curious and cruel crowd. Their opposition was disturbing, but they were not the greatest threat to his cause. That lay in the halfhearted support of those whom he had counted upon to carry his message throughout the world. It was the disciples and the others who had promised to follow him who were able most grievously to wound him. He needed their support. He was eager to claim their loyal devotion.

Christ still thirsts for evidence that we are seriously concerned to tell others the good news which he brought to the world. Without such devotion all life is in grave danger, but with it a new and better civilization will grow out of the ashes of the old world.

Prayer

Help us this day, O Lord, to take up our cross and follow the Christ who died on Calvary. Help us to speak words of faith and assurance to victims of sin. Use us to spread the good news of thy love for all mankind. Give us courage to do the hardest things when they will help to advance thy kingdom. With it all, make us worthy of thy love and receptive to the incoming of thy Holy Spirit. In Jesus' name. Amen.

SEVENTH DAY

Faith Demands Service

Scripture: Read Mark 9:38-50

IT IS A STIRRING EXPERIENCE TO RECAPTURE THE EVENTS WHICH occurred during the earthly life of Jesus. Pilgrims to Palestine endeavor to recover something of Jesus' presence by living for a time in the places made sacred by his earthly ministry. Others, unable to cross the seas to Palestine, faithfully observe periods of meditation when they seek to understand more clearly the meaning of the Cross.

After a Christian has lived again the events of the Crucifixion, he is pursued to the end of his days by the drama of Calvary. He is moved to horror by the crass cruelty of those charged with the duty of the execution. He is hushed into silence by the awesome spectacle of tragedy. Every word which Jesus utters has power to stir his deepest feelings.

"I thirst!" The lips of the Master form the words. In imagination we stand at the foot of the cross. We tell ourselves again and again that we would never have allowed the tragedy to happen; if we had been there, we would have rushed forward to give the Master a drink of water. Such a conclusion is worthy. Of course we would not have been deaf to the Saviour's cry.

But recall another and earlier occasion when Jesus was talking to his disciples. It was near the end of his ministry. He was showing what it meant to be one of his followers. He talked of the hungry, the imprisoned, the sick, and *the thirsty*. Then he reminded his listeners that one who serves a needy individual serves Christ himself. He said, "Inasmuch as ye have done it unto one of the least of these my brethren, ye have done it unto me."

The cry of Jesus from the cross is an eternal reminder of the sobbing plea for help which rises unceasingly from the parched lips and tortured minds of those who are in need. Every follower of Jesus can and must respond to the call of Christ for aid. We serve him whenever we bring relief to those in physical pain, in mental anguish, or in spiritual distress.

Prayer

We thank thee, O God, for the opportunity to serve thee by serving thy children. Our hearts are moved by a longing to help the crucified Lord. Teach us to hear his plea for aid in the cries which come from the needy of our world. Give us the joy of knowing that we lift the load from thy heart whenever we lift the load of thy children. Accept the dedication of our lives to thee. In Jesus' name. Amen.

SIXTH WEEK

"It Is Finished."
             —*John 19:30*

FIRST DAY

The Finished Work of Christ

Scripture: Read John 19:30-42

FROM OUR VANTAGE POINT, CENTURIES AWAY FROM THE EVENT, we recognize the triumph of the Cross. But the friends of Jesus who watched the unfolding drama saw it as stark tragedy. The kingly qualities in the Master were in evidence when he lifted the curtain to let the repentant thief see his place in heaven. The other utterances of Jesus had given hints that someone extraordinary was facing death.

Then came the Sixth Word! The voice of Jesus throbbed with triumphant assurance. "It is finished!" he cried.

What was finished on Calvary? A great life? Indeed, that was not finished. The influence of the earthly life of Jesus would continue in every century through the work of his followers. Did this mark the end of his teaching and healing ministry? No, men and women would be his voice to spread his gospel throughout the world. They would be his hands to heal the sick, the maimed, and the blind.

Scholars in every century have tried to tell us what was accomplished by the sacrifice which Christ made on Calvary. All the theories of the Atonement stem from this dramatic moment in history.

Some argue that divine justice demanded a price sufficient to balance the cost of human sin. Christ's death on the cross, they say, provided that balance. The cry "It is finished" is the

109

acknowledgment that the debt for humanity had been paid.

The directness of this point of view makes it appealing. But it perpetuates the legalism of the Old Testament. Jesus did not come to the earth merely to satisfy a legal situation. He came to awaken the souls of men to the glory of God's eternal love. He came to call each of us from sin to repentance.

From the time when men first chose evil instead of good, God had yearned for his people to return to him. Sin makes God a stranger. It erects a barrier between the heavenly Father and his children.

A man finds it difficult to pray when he is living an evil life; he discovers, finally, that God has slipped out of his thinking. For a time he is satisfied to be free of the obligations which faith makes necessary. But at last the night comes! A loved one dies; sudden tragedy strikes; security is lost; sickness hounds him. Night comes! And man is lonely and afraid! He longs to recapture the awareness of the divine presence which once had seemed so real. But he is lost. His sin has carried him so far from the rock of faith that he feels God is far away.

That was the experience of the people whose story is told in the Old Testament. It is the experience also of many of us in the twentieth century. God did not leave the Hebrew people without a way of salvation. Through the voices of the prophets he had pleaded again and again for their return. Many of the voices were tender and appealing. "The Lord thy God in the midst of thee is mighty," said Zephaniah; "he will save, he will rejoice over thee with joy; he will rest in his love, he will joy over thee with singing."

Neither the harsh demands of Micah nor the tender assurances of Zephaniah were sufficient. Salvation required a witness of unique power and influence.

That witness came in the one who died on Calvary. All of us bow in humility when we become aware of the depth of the heavenly Father's love. In Christ he completed the plan of salvation by which we are restored to a rightful place as his children.

Prayer

We give thanks unto thee, O Lord, for the saving power which came to mankind through Christ. We recall with gratitude when thy hand in Christ lifted us out of the morass of evil which had claimed us. Our salvation is in him. Make us thy witnesses to tell others of the one who on Calvary opened the door to a life free from sin. In Jesus' name. Amen.

SECOND DAY

The Unfinished Work of Christ

Scripture: Read John 17:1-13

THE NEW TESTAMENT STORY INDICATES THAT JOHN WAS THE only one of the twelve who was present during the trying hours of the Crucifixion. The disciples accepted the Sixth Word. Ever since Jesus had been dragged before the high priest, they had been telling one another that all was finished. They needed no one to remind them that the end of life for their Master was at hand. With his death they were ready to assume the collapse of all the hopes and dreams which had made those last years so satisfying.

An Eastern legend declares that Alexander the Great gave orders before his death that his hands were to be left out of the casket when he was carried to the grave. It was his desire

111

that all his subjects should see that the hands were empty; that he, who possessed the world's richest treasures of gold and silver, went to his final resting place without any of his wealth.

The disciples were persuaded that the death of Jesus marked the end of all their dreams. They concluded that it was unnecessary for them to be with him during those grueling hours on Calvary to be certain that he was taking nothing with him and was leaving nothing behind except the heartbreaks and disappointments of his friends.

At the beginning of his ministry the close followers of Jesus were convinced that he would achieve great victories—perhaps in the material and political realms—but certainly spiritual victories. They had watched with misgivings the growing opposition to his message. Even in Galilee, where they were accustomed to large and enthusiastic crowds, the unfriendly attitude seemed to be growing. They found it difficult to understand Jesus when he told them he was going up to Jerusalem to be crucified. They fondly looked to the day when the common people would rise up to proclaim him the expected Messiah.

On Monday of Holy Week, Judas had decided that all was finished unless Jesus could be forced to call upon divine resources to dispose of his enemies. Strong arguments can be gathered to support those who believe Judas betrayed his Master only because he was certain Jesus would summon miraculous powers to help him.

But the arrest and conviction of the Master seemed to mark the end. "It is finished!" they said one to another. The hope of the Kingdom was gone. Fear for their personal safety kept the disciples from standing vigil at the cross. They realized that the Jewish authorities were ready to use their influence to destroy anyone or anything which savored of the Nazarene. But perhaps it was not so much personal fear as an overwhelming sense of defeat which drove them away from Jerusalem that day. The record suggests that some of them scurried back to Galilee to take up the broken threads of their lives. They went back to the fishing boats where they had first heard the challenge to follow Jesus.

These men soon learned that they were mistaken. Something was finished on Calvary, but it was not their Christ, nor was it his dream of the Kingdom.

It is never wise to mark the end of a worthy cause in a moment when its enemies appear to have triumphed. God's victories are often in the making at the very time when hope and courage seem to have lost the battle.

Prayer

Too often, O Lord, we are guilty of believing that Christ suffered the defeat of his cause on Calvary. We act as if the forces which destroyed him had triumphed. We still affirm that hatred and political power and material might are supreme. Forgive us. Help us live with the understanding that nothing is finished until it is in keeping with thy will. In Jesus' name. Amen.

THIRD DAY

The Unfinished Aspirations of the Soul

Scripture: Read Matt. 20:17-29

THE WOMEN WHO HAD BEEN WITH JESUS THROUGHOUT THE trying agony of the Cross had prayed for a speedy termination

113

of his suffering. When he said, "It is finished!" they breathed a sigh of relief. A great load was lifted from their hearts when they knew that his torture and agony were coming to an end.

The words might have had a deeper significance if they had been able to ponder the matter from every viewpoint. But their interest was absorbed by the pitiable plight of the one they loved. They had intently watched his every move; their emotions had been stirred by each of his Words. They longed to be able to do something to help him.

When at last he said, "It is finished!" they must have experienced an overwhelming sense of relief. Even death was better than a continuation of the agony of those hours.

Christians often comfort one another during periods of grief by the reminder that death has brought release from suffering. To help a victim of sorrow to understand that the one he loves is better off now that his pain is over is sometimes the most comforting service which a sympathetic friend can render. The sense of separation and the inevitable loneliness which will come in the months ahead are minimized by the realization that the beloved is no longer in pain.

It was that way with the women at Calvary. Each of them had a deep affection for the Master. His mother, Mary Magdalene, and the wife of Cleophas had followed him even when his ministry took him away from the familiar hills of Galilee. They had journeyed with him when he came down to Jerusalem for the last time. They would miss him during the months ahead. They felt a personal loss which made that hour the darkest period they had ever known. They were not thinking of themselves at that time; their thoughts were for the one hanging on the cross. They were intensely aware of his physical agony. They were willing to welcome death because it meant that his pain was at an end.

"It is finished!" These words of Jesus sent a wave of relief across the little band which had been faithful to him. It was the end—the end of suffering. It was not better for them but better for him.

Too often death seems the worst thing which can happen to a loved one or to a friend. We tend to mark all of life by whether the heart keeps pumping within the body.

Such an attitude is foreign to one who is imbued by the Christian faith. Christians never measure the length of life by the number of years one has lived on the earth. To say that life is finished because the earthly span has been reached is to deny the revelation which God gave to the world in Jesus Christ.

We can say "it is finished" to describe the completion of an earthly existence. The words may imply either relief or regret, depending upon the quality of the life which is coming to an end. But such words do not take into consideration the hope which burns in the heart of a faithful Christian.

When life on earth is finished, we are merely ending one phase of human existence. There is heaven ahead! Eternal aspirations are never finished.

Prayer

We are grateful, O God, for the faithfulness to thee which marks the lives of many of thy children. Our own weakness is made real when we remember the small company of followers who kept vigil at the cross. We have too often turned from thee to the world to find our satisfactions. We have lived as if the influence and power of Christ were finished. Keep us alive to the truth which never fails. Use us that the work of Jesus may continue to be accomplished in the hearts of men. In his name we pray. Amen.

FOURTH DAY

The Satisfactions of Work Well Done

Scripture: Read John 3:1-21

IT IS NOT DIFFICULT TO UNDERSTAND WHAT THESE BRIEF WORDS meant to Jesus. They meant the end of his suffering. His life and his work on earth were finished.

There is a suggestion here that Jesus was satisfied that his mission was completed. The work was done. That does not mean that he had accomplished all he had set out to do. He had preached the good news with the expectation that people would respond. He wanted men everywhere to repent of the crass selfishness which was the enemy of the soul.

The Master's work seems unfinished if we look merely at the disappointing response of many of his listeners. But in his death on the cross his work was completed. He had set out upon a breath-taking adventure when he began to preach the good news of the Kingdom. The immediate response in Galilee had been gratifying. But there came a day when only the gift of life itself could accomplish what his words had failed to do. From that day "he steadfastly set his face to go to Jerusalem." It was not an easy course, but he did not waver from it.

The Sixth Word may be spoken by anyone who has steadfastly persevered in a worthy course. "I have fought a good fight; . . . I have kept the faith," the apostle Paul wrote during the closing hours of his life. If the end brought feelings

116

of regret, they were softened by the consciousness that he had done his best.

The early work of Christian missions in the Fiji Islands took the lives of many noble men. Bishop Freeman Patterson was killed in revenge for the wrongs committed by white traders against the natives; John Williams fell before the clubs of savages on the island of Eromanga; Thomas Baker was killed by cannibal mountaineers. Yet twenty-five years after the first missionaries landed on the island, the Martyr's Church was erected. It stands as a memorial to those who gave their all for the faith. On a plaque inside the door of the church these words are inscribed: "They finished their work in the Lord Jesus."

Some will wonder how these sturdy souls "finished their work in the Lord Jesus" when they died as young men at the hands of savages who did not understand their mission. Yet a life is always finished when it has been lived with an unfailing dedication to noble goals.

The New Testament was introduced into Spain through the labors of a man named Juliano Hernandez. He was sentenced to death by burning. At his trial the judge said, "I fear you are throwing yourself into the fire, and for what?" Hernandez responded triumphantly: "For the joy of bringing food to the perishing, water to the thirsty, light to those that sit in darkness, rest to the weary and heavy laden. Sir, I have counted the cost, and I will pay the price."

Many followers of Jesus were convinced that he threw his life away when he went to the cross. They saw no possibility that enduring values would result from his death. Jesus had counted the cost, and he willingly paid the price. He could say with justification, "It is finished!" The purpose of his life, which was also the purpose of his heavenly Father, had been fulfilled.

Christians will always be challenged by the Sixth Word. Because of what happened on Calvary, we will never be satisfied until we have lived out our days with courageous devotion to high and worthy ends. To produce such lives is one of the reasons why Christ died on the cross. Then we too can say: "It is finished!"

Prayer

Our lives are incomplete, O Lord, until we shape every thought and desire according to thy purpose and thy will. Help us today to accept the hope which broke through the dark despair of the first Calvary. Because Christ died on the cross, thou art forever our Father, yearning for us to be faithful to the best that is in us. We are humbled by thy love. Strengthen us by thy presence that we may not fail in all we do to reflect our high calling as thy children. In Jesus' name we pray. Amen.

FIFTH DAY

The Persuasiveness of Suffering

Scripture: Read John 12:23-36

THE PERSPECTIVE WHICH COMES WITH THE YEARS MAKES IT easy for us to declare that, from the beginning, Christ was destined to die on the cross. Old Testament references to the expected Messiah as a "man of sorrows, and acquainted with grief" readily apply to the one who suffered on Calvary. Yet there were other references by the prophets which indicated that the Messiah's coming would be greeted with joy, that he would be heard gladly by a people who needed only his witness to persuade them to return to God.

Jesus taught and healed. He called men to repentance. He sent out seventy faithful men to extend the influence of his ministry. It is evident that he labored with the expectation that hosts of people would accept him as the Christ. And why not? Where in history has God given such a witness as we find in the one who healed the sick, preached the Sermon on the Mount, put the divine seal of approval upon little children, upon womanhood, and upon the lives of the most humble of men?

When the fires of opposition to his message blazed high, it became evident to him, before it became evident to his disciples, that teaching and healing were not enough. Sacrificial death was necessary if the frozen heart of man was to be melted.

There were few in his circle of followers who believed that he could accomplish his purpose by dying on the cross. That should not seem strange to people who live in the twentieth century, for there are still millions of the followers of Jesus who refuse to believe that the Kingdom can be brought about through sacrifice. We still want to flourish our swords and shout our invectives against those who differ from us in attitudes or beliefs.

God knew better than men what power was available through suffering, and Christ understood the heart of his Father. Because of that knowledge he gladly, even triumphantly, welcomed the end. "And I, if I be lifted up from the earth, will draw all men unto me," he said in explaining to his disciples what the Cross would accomplish. The uplifted Christ would indelibly print a picture in the hearts of men of a

119

a God who suffers in their behalf. Life would be forever holy because of the Cross; sin would always seem vile and sordid because of the events on Calvary.

His confident faith in the plan of his Father led Jesus to accept the condemnation of the crowd, the petty scheming of the Jewish authorities, the temporizing of Pilate, the cruelty of the soldiers, and the physical torture of the Crucifixion. Every step of the way up to Calvary and every moment on the cross brought the divine purpose closer to realization. When the end of the suffering was at hand, Jesus was able to say triumphantly, "It is finished!" The work was done. Man would always know that God loves him and had offered him the way back from degradation to the spiritual heights.

Prayer

Open our eyes this day, O God, to the Cross as a way to win mankind to thy cause. Forgive us for our reliance upon power and influence as the best means to get what we want from life. Help us to learn the meaning of sacrifice. We offer our lives to thee, seeking to let the spirit of Jesus direct all that we do. If it be a cross which is demanded of us, help us to accept it. So shall thy name be glorified through us. In Jesus' name. Amen.

SIXTH DAY

God's Witness from the Cross

Scripture: Read John 14:15-31

WE ALL NEED THE WITNESS OF THE CROSS. WE CONTINUE TO choose evil instead of good. By our neglect we still allow the presence of God to fade from our lives. We often are so completely absorbed with physical satisfactions and material desires that we lose an awareness of eternal truth.

Within the Christian faith there have been those who were persuaded that salvation is found by other means than by faith in the God who was revealed by the crucified Christ. The ancient sage who sat for years on a pole to avoid the taint of the world was a forerunner of a host of men and women who believe that salvation is found by going apart from the world, by torturing the body, or by the harsh discipline of endless hours of prayer and meditation.

There are values in seclusion or in separation from the pleasures of the world. Our heritage has been enriched by the influence of those who have subjected their bodies to harsh disciplines. But salvation does not depend upon such practices. Calvary makes it unnecessary for us to grope blindly in order to gain the assurance that God loves us.

The major reasons for despair and fear were abolished that day at the cross! The way of salvation was clearly marked for all of us to see and to know. Paul could say, "The life which I now live in the flesh I live by the faith of the Son of God, who loved me, and gave himself for me." The Cross was the means by which Paul was brought back to the Father. In it he saw the completion of the divine plan of salvation.

Often the benefits of the Cross are neglected because the message appears too good to be true. Some of us still refuse to believe that the tentacles of sin have been broken by the power which radiates from the crucified Christ.

H. G. Wells told of a man who tumbled down a mountain slope into a kingdom where everyone was blind. Instead of accepting the man's tale of his ability to see, the people charged him with lying and misrepresentation. When he finally convinced them that he possessed the gift of sight, they pitied him. Their leaders prepared to perform an operation which would reduce him to their own state of blindness. They thought blindness would save him from stumbling in the dark.

There is a kingdom of the blind in the spiritual realm. When a pilgrim wanders into this world with face aglow, announcing that Christ has brought him light, many turn away in self-righteous superiority. Such a thing couldn't be true, they reason. "We are blind so why should not others be blind?" they say.

A light came to the world during the first century which is sufficient for all of the ages. It burns brightest when our needs are most pressing. It offers a full and complete plan by which evil can be conquered. God's witness was completed that afternoon on Calvary.

Prayer

Dear God and Father of us all, we bow in humility before the miracle of the Cross. The way of salvation through faith in Christ has sometimes seemed too wonderful to be true. We have sought a harder way. Help us put our trust in the one whose sacrifice revealed the eternal love which is in thy heart. Save us from fruitless efforts to seek assurance by our own strivings. As we pause to look again toward Calvary, give us a willingness to accept the miracle of thy love. So shall we find peace and courage to live nobly according to thy will. In Jesus' name. Amen.

SEVENTH DAY

The Certainty of God's Great Love
Scripture: Read Rom. 5:1-11

THE CROSS MARKED THE BEGINNING OF A NEW WORLD ERA. THE old doubts were banished. Men found a Saviour. "All my life I have been seeking to climb out of the pit of my besetting sins," said Seneca. "And I can't do it: and I never will, unless a hand is let down to me to draw me up." The miracle for which the pagan philosopher prayed occurred in Palestine. The Cross enabled men to see the hand of God reaching down to lift them out of the vale of despair and fear.

Addressing a medical association, Dr. James MacKenzie, the eminent British heart specialist, said: "Get a hold on what your Saviour's death should mean to you, and your lives as medical men will become enlarged and enriched."

The same is true for all of us. The Cross puts a seal of nobility upon every life. It gives new stature to those who are crippled by anxiety. It reveals the God who loves men enough to allow his Son to die upon the cross. Such love makes him personal and available and loving. It led William Wilberforce to cry out to one who was justifying slavery: "How can you say such things about men for whom Christ died?"

Only a few in the crowd which surged around the cross understood the meaning of the events which transpired that day. For the most part they were satisfied to observe or to criticize or even to weep. In this generation there are those who want to make a minor thing of the Crucifixion. But what happened that day has changed the course of history. Men were freed from enslavement to sin.

Lady Jane Grey of Scotland maintained a remarkable calm when she was sentenced to die. She spent the evening before her execution writing to loved ones and friends. One of her letters included these triumphant words: "Fight manfully on. Come life, come death, the loss of men is not the loss of the cause. The battle is God's; the victory is His."

Lady Jane Grey's confident faith had its foundation in the Cross. She is one of an unnumbered host who discovered the answer to their deepest needs in the revelation of God in Christ. Before Calvary men were uncertain whether the struggle with sin could result in victory; whether the injustices and cruelties of the world could be righted.

Calvary made a supreme difference for us and for people in every age. It offers freedom by the miracle of faith; it promises release from the world's harrowing misery if we are willing to accept the God who was revealed in Christ.

"It is finished!" The work of salvation is complete. It remains for us to accept the good news and to pattern our lives after the one who chose to be the servant of all and to die that we might be certain of God's great love.

Prayer

Dear Father, we praise thee for thy works of creation. We glorify thy name for the sustaining power which is evident in the nature of our world. Our gratitude is deepest when we remember the provision for our salvation which was made by the events which occurred on Calvary. Help us this day to accept thy gift of love as it was given to us in Christ. By thy grace help us to be worthy. In Jesus' name. Amen.

SEVENTH WEEK

"Father, into Thy Hands
I Commend My Spirit"
—Luke 23:46

FIRST DAY

Committing Life to God

Scripture: Read Luke 23:46-56

THE DEATH OF JESUS CAME UNEXPECTEDLY FOR MANY IN THE crowd which waited around the cross. They had not looked for death to claim its victim so soon. They were accustomed to crucifixions and were prepared to stay throughout the day and into the night before witnessing the end of the physical torture. Victims of crucifixions often hung for more than twenty-four hours before their weakened bodies gave up the struggle for life.

The unique nature of Jesus was in control on Calvary as it had been on many occasions when merely human reactions might have dictated a different course. He had always held his body under magnificent control; he had it under control here. He welcomed death as a friendly release from the ravages of pain.

His final word was one of commitment: "Father, into thy hands I commend my spirit." Both the Son of man and the Son of God could say those words. His attitude reflected the complete surrender of his life and spirit to God.

The final words of Jesus are the New Testament version of a passage in the thirty-first psalm. The psalmist declared, "Into thine hand I commit my spirit." It remained for Jesus to preface those words with the term "Father." The psalmist directs his words to the "Lord," or to the "Lord God of truth." Jesus thought of God as more personal, more loving, and more deeply concerned with the affairs of men.

In the First Word spoken on Calvary and in the Final Word Jesus used intimate and endearing terms which were familiar to the family. The experience of crucifixion began and ended with a reminder that his Father had not deserted him in the hour of need.

We need this final witness of Christ as he hung on the cross. The commitment of our life is often to shoddy things. We place our confidence in money or in material goods. We struggle for social position as if that in itself could insure our happiness. Our commitment is too often to the things of the world.

While I was speaking on a college campus, a Chinese student asked for a personal conference. In response to my questions he told me he was taking an engineering course with a major in chemistry. He declared that he wanted to learn everything available about weapons and explosives. I was surprised to learn that he had been brought up in a Christian family in his homeland. I inquired whether as a follower of Jesus he felt that China needed guns and explosives more than skills which might be constructive. He was as blunt as the inborn courtesy of the Chinese could allow him to be. "China needs to be strong if she is to take her rightful place in the world," he said. "I am going to give my life to help her."

Many of us find it easy to dismiss the need to commit our lives to Christ. We are persuaded that surrender to worldliness promises more immediate satisfactions.

Jesus left an example of what a dedicated life ought to be. He committed his all to God. We too must practice the discipline by which we give ourselves to the heavenly Father.

128

The answer to our deepest personal problems, as well as those of our world, await such a surrender of life to him.

Prayer

Dear Father, we thank thee for the example of Jesus. When we remember the commitment of his efforts to thee, our own weaknesses make us ashamed. Help us this day to use all we have wisely and well and then to leave the rest to thy loving care. Let thy Holy Spirit give us strength to do thy will. In Jesus' name. Amen.

SECOND DAY

Faith's Answer to Despair

Scripture: Read John 1:1-14

THE ROMAN TYRANTS HAD DONE THEIR WORK. PILATE HAD condemned Christ to death; his soldiers had carried out the sentence. They had shown their scorn for the gentle Galilean by a hastily made sign which was nailed above his head. "The King of the Jews!" it announced. They had gambled for his clothing. No act of ridicule was too low if it added scorn to the victim of their torture.

Furthermore, the foremost religious leaders were gloating with satisfaction. The depth of their hatred had been evident throughout the hours while Jesus was hanging on the cross. They had hurled invectives at him, "wagging their heads, and saying, Thou that destroyest the temple, and buildest it in three days, save thyself. If thou be the Son of God, come down from the cross."

129

The chief priests and the scribes had remained on Calvary to make certain nothing happened to interfere with the Crucifixion. They cried out in derision, "He saved others; himself he cannot save. If he be the King of Israel, let him now come down from the cross, and we will believe him." They had missed completely the revelation of God which was unfolding before their eyes.

The common people were victims of mass hysteria. Only a few days before, many of them had joined the pilgrims from every part of Judea and Galilee in hailing the man from Nazareth as King. But their enthusiasm cooled quickly under the pressure of the false tesimony of the temple authorities. Their acclaim changed first to sullen silence and then to outspoken opposition. Duped by false leaders, they failed to realize that the eternal destiny of man was in the making.

Even the close friends of Jesus had forsaken him. The disciples, whom he had counted upon to spread his teachings, could not be seen in the crowd. Their fear did not allow them even to mingle unknown with the mob; they were skulking far away in furtive silence, hoping no one would recognize them as followers of the Nazarene.

Through all this tense drama the gentle man from Galilee suffered humanity's supreme physical agony. It is said that during the Middle Ages instruments of death were more painful and brought death more slowly than the cross. Yet man has probably never devised a form of torture more painful.

Who can look upon the events which unfolded that day without sensing that the world had come to one of its most wretched hours? Infamy, hatred, greed, cruelty—these were the qualities which ruled the passions and deeds of men. When we attempt to recapture the state of the political and religious world of that day, when we recall the disappointing reaction of the common people and the followers of Jesus, it is easy to characterize the whole situation. If we were asked to describe the nature of the world at that moment, we could easily give the answer which the editors of a Washington newspaper gave to a young reader who had asked them to describe what our century is like. We would say, "The world is disappointing! Tragic! Terrible!"

That was not the answer of Jesus. Listen again to his words. Standing by the cross, we can see that the end is close at hand. As the lips of the Master move, we step forward a little closer and cup our ears. These are not words of defeat. They hold no rebuke for his enemies. "Father, into thy hands I commend my spirit," he whispers. That is all! When the final syllable has been uttered, he takes his last breath. The end has come!

Prayer

Dear Father, help us this day to realize what the Cross cost thee in pain in order that we may know thy love. Forgive us if we accept too easily the manifestations of thine eternal concern for thy children. Keep us faithful lest we take our place with those who brought Jesus to his death. The miracle which occurred on Calvary will forever change our attitudes and our actions. Accept our dedication to that which is holy. In Jesus' name. Amen.

THIRD DAY

Trusting God's Love and Mercy

Scripture: Read Matt. 7:21-29

THE FINAL WORD OF JESUS SUGGESTS THE ONLY SATISFYING answer to the complex problems of our world. It not only points the way, but it gives an example of how a practicing Christian can meet stark and unrelieved tragedy today.

Each of us confronts certain moments when it appears that life has gone awry. A survey of the world out yonder or the world enclosed by our personal problems and interests leads many of us to decide that life is unpleasant, difficult, and frightening. In such an hour it is easy to strike out in anger against those who have contributed to this condition. Sometimes we bewail our fate and decide that providence has been unfair.

Those were the possibilities which faced Jesus. If he was tempted to yield to such thoughts, he did not do so. Instead he offered all of us the open doorway to peace within and to triumph without. He committed his life and work to his heavenly Father, confident that God would give direction to the future as he had to the past.

Jesus lived during a period when the interest of many people throughout the world was absorbed with the problem of freedom. They were dominated by an aggressive, enslaving tyrant. Rome had extended its harsh rule over a large part of the earth. The message of Jesus had been weighed by the Jews with a supreme question on their minds. They had wondered if he was the promised Messiah who would restore the lost grandeur of Israel. Everything he said and did was weighed in the balance to discover whether it gave hope that his people might escape the burden imposed by the oppressor.

Blind patriots were offended by him, for he did not offer leadership in a revolutionary uprising. He taught men that release from bondage lay in the realm of the spirit. He went so far as to suggest that they "render to Caesar the things that are Caesar's." He was concerned with the restoration of man's lost awareness of God. He affirmed that other matters would fall naturally into their proper place if people were in accord with the purposes of their heavenly Father.

Civilization in the twentieth century is torn by international dissensions. Millions of people are victims of anxieties and fears. Others are physically and mentally weakened by an even more dangerous quality—an overwhelming hatred of those outside their national frontiers. Suspicion shapes their waking thoughts and warps their dreams.

It is here that the example of Jesus offers the way to peace. Jesus was faced with international tensions at least as serious as those of our day. His example challenges us to "love one another: as I have loved you." He did not rage against his Roman enemies, nor did he scourge them with threats. He left judgment to a higher power.

The solution of the problems which threaten to engulf us in the twentieth century awaits the time when all of us are willing to lay our disagreements and our anxieties before God. Calmness of mind and international security can be realized if we are willing to say: "Father, into thy hands I commend my spirit."

Jesus was no robed figure seated upon a throne; he was a

man bleeding and sweating under the scorching heat of a noonday sun. In that extremity his Last Word was not a cry of anguish, but a ringing affirmation. He placed his trust in divine grace and mercy.

Our lives will be enriched if we are willing to give our best to serve God's purposes in the world and then commit the rest to him.

Prayer

Dear Father, we are often bewildered and discouraged by what life has brought us. Sorrow and pain give food to our doubts. Thy face is blurred and dim. We give thanks for the Christ who died on Calvary. His sacrifice becomes a challenge in our moments of weakness. His trust rebukes our doubts. Let the Spirit of Christ strengthen our faith as we do our work this day. May our trust in thy goodness be deepened when we remember the way he placed his life in thy hands. In Jesus' name. Amen.

FOURTH DAY

Dedicating All of Life to God

Scripture: Read John 5:17-31

TO COMMIT LIFE TO GOD IS STILL OUR BEST ANSWER TO THE bewildering uncertainty which sometimes overwhelms us during hours of pain or sickness. Alice Bretz discovered that truth during a tragic experience. She was the wife of a New Jersey physician, enjoying her home, her garden, and her friends. Life seemed rich and satisfying until she was stricken with a disease which robbed her of her sight. The tragedy did not come suddenly; it developed after painful operations and long periods in crowded hospitals. She wrote after total blindness had come upon her, "I've gone as far as possible, and then put the way to God. His help has never failed." Mrs. Bretz learned what many other sufferers have learned—that healing for the mind is available to those who will commit their way to God, who will put their trust in him.

No moment in human experience is more difficult than the utter loneliness which engulfs one who has lost someone near and dear to him. Life loses its meaning. Grief lays him low, and he feels he cannot rise again. It is tempting then to rage against the injustices which seem to dominate his life. Any human being is pitiful when he meets death without an awareness of God.

The Cross is man's best witness for such an hour. Jesus faced death. He was standing at the edge of eternity when he spoke the Seventh Word. In that moment he committed his life and spirit to his Father with unfailing confidence in divine love and mercy. "Father, into thy hands I commend my spirit," he whispered. In Christ's example we find the open door to an experience of triumphant hope.

The Seventh Word must be considered in the light of the total ministry of Jesus. He had already given his time and strength to realize God's purposes in the world. He was not committing his spirit as a final gesture of desperation. His whole life had been consecrated to God.

There is something disappointing about a person who, without penitence, looks to the heavenly Father for mercy in the hour of death when his entire life has been dominated by selfish greed. It is pitiful to observe a family which gathers for a funeral service, hoping to hear words assuring them that the soul of the one they love has found a home in heaven, when they have never made any attempt previously to do God's will. In the hour of death they have called for the services of a pastor who is a stranger. They are willing to trust the spirit of their beloved to God in death, but they refuse to dedicate themselves to him in life.

The Final Word of Jesus on the cross was a seal upon what had been his lifelong dedication. From the vantage point of experience we learn here the wisdom of a consecrated life. It is our privilege to commend our spirits to God in childhood, in youth, and in maturity, as well as in the hour when eternal hope seems more important than worldly satisfactions.

Prayer

Our strivings have left us dissatisfied, O God. Our best efforts have often ended in defeat. We are discouraged by the emptiness which follows our labors. We need thee. We need the confidence which comes from the knowledge that thy plans are eternal. Help us to trust thee more. Enable us courageously to do our best and then to leave it all in thy hands. In Jesus' name. Amen.

FIFTH DAY

Learning the Lesson of Surrender
Scripture: Read John 15:15-27

THE SEVENTH WORD WAS SPOKEN IN THE LAST MOMENT BEFORE death brought an end to the cruel spectacle of crucifixion. It voices ultimate truth. There was no time then for speculation

136

or reasoning. What was said at that point was supremely significant.

"Father, into thy hands I commend my spirit," Jesus said. The important emphasis was upon God. It told good news about the heavenly Father. It announced that he is worthy of trust, not a harsh and cruel tyrant. It reminds us that he is not a haughty ruler who is blind to human need; he is like a father, always close at hand; he is a God who can be trusted.

Throughout the centuries this assurance has lifted the fainting heart of man. We often feel alone and forsaken. We often wonder whether cruel fate has taken the place of divine providence in the affairs of men. We often speculate whether virtue will eventually fall victim to the greedy march of evil. Whenever our eyes look upon the cross, we know that a dependable witness is proclaiming a sure foundation for assurance and hope. We are reminded that God is a Father who can be trusted, that life is at its best when it is committed to him.

The final answer of Jesus to the tragedy in which he was involved was not a curse upon his enemies, nor a rebuff to the people who failed to understand what it meant for him to sacrifice his life in their behalf. His Final Word was an example, a stirring challenge for all the ages to follow. When sorrow had taken its toll, when pain had reaped its worst, when death had crept up to the cross to claim him, he lifted his eyes toward heaven. His weakening voice was then merely a whisper, "Father, into thy hands I commend my spirit."

We will never climb the heights which God makes it possible for us to reach until we learn the lesson of surrender. We are expected to do our best with life. It is admirable when we face our opportunities with courage. A businessman has complex problems to face. The factory worker has moments of discouragement when life seems meaningless. The student

137

finds himself pursued by doubts about the enduring values of his efforts.

All of us experience moments of frustration and defeat. They will prove too great a load to bear unless we learn the lesson of surrender. Life is made different if, having done our best, we leave the results of our efforts to God.

Prayer

Teach us to trust thee more, O God. We are weak when we try to live by our own strength. Our strivings leave us disappointed until we are willing to leave the results in thy hands. Forgive us for our lack of faith. Accept our dedication of the present and the future to thee. Whatever use thou canst make of our efforts, they are thine. In Jesus' name. Amen.

SIXTH DAY

Discovering the Secrets of Commitment
Scripture: Read Heb. 11:32-40

THE FINAL COMMITMENT WHICH JESUS MADE TO GOD IS NOT A solitary event which stands out like a beacon in a life which contradicts it. Wherever the spotlight of attention focuses upon the Master, we find him talking of his Father, rendering service in the name of his Father, or putting his life on the scales in behalf of his Father. The whole of the Master's ministry was a testimony of his complete dedication to God.

Recall Luke's account of Jesus' words in the temple when he was a boy of twelve. "Wist ye not that I must be about my Father's business?" Jesus asked. In his earliest years, perhaps at his mother's knee, he had learned that God wanted his life

138

to be lived for him. The carpenter shop was important as a means of livelihood, but it did not blind him to the responsibility which he felt to do his Father's will. Even as a boy his life belonged to God.

The commitment was reaffirmed during the testing days of the temptation experience. He saw before him the wealth and honor of the world. "All these things will I give thee, if thou wilt fall down and worship me," was the promise which was given if he would yield to evil. Jesus turned away from the glory of the world. He was determined that spiritual values should have first claim upon his time and strength.

If any question remained about his motive and purpose, it was made dramatically clear during the Sermon on the Mount. He reminded his listeners that "ye cannot serve God and mammon." He summoned them to "seek first the kingdom of God and his righteousness; and all these things shall be added unto you." He challenged the crowd on the mountainside to make the same dedication which he himself had already made. He was serving God instead of mammon; he was seeking first the kingdom of God and his righteousness. The Sermon on the Mount, apart from its matchless teaching, is a vital witness of faith. It presents a portrait of one whose life was entirely surrendered to God and who would be forever restless until others shared his spirit.

The commitment of all of life to his heavenly Father was again demonstrated in the Garden of Gethsemane. The Cross already appeared as an immediate and terrifying reality! There had been talk of death, but now it was actually at hand. Jesus revealed in a sudden moment of insight the longings of his own heart. "Father," he prayed, "if thou be willing, remove this cup from me." He did not want to die. Those who make the Cross a beautiful symbol of divine love, without understanding the scorching tears and the withering pain which were involved, do violence to the witness of God in Christ. The Cross was not a painting to be gazed upon, nor a crucifix to be fingered and admired. It was life at its worst. We understand why Jesus should have wanted to avoid it.

He did not tarry long with pleas for escape. His request for release was prefaced by the words: "If it be thy will." It was quickly followed by a complete surrender of his own desires: "Nevertheless not my will, but thine, be done."

The Seventh Word was not an unrelated evidence of consecration. It was a dramatic summary, with his last breath, of what had been the attitude of Jesus in every moment of his life. It was as if he looked down the ages during that final minute to see his followers struggling with the problems of living and dying. His example revealed the only attitude which can satisfy our spiritual longings. To commit himself to God was the daily custom of Jesus; he knew no other way. He made use of the last moment on the cross to declare for all time the triumphant power of a surrendered life.

Who can look upon this final act of dedication without being changed? Our hearts are stirred by a desire to use our lives for God.

Prayer

Heavenly Father, we thank thee for the example of commitment which Jesus gave us on the cross. His attitude is a rebuke to our selfishness. We are humbled by his willingness to leave everything in thy hands. Too often we insist upon getting our way. Forgive us for our thoughts of self. Help us to walk today with thee, using wisely thy gifts, then leaving what is accomplished in thy care. In Jesus' name. Amen.

SEVENTH DAY

Finding Heaven at the End

Scripture: Read Eph. 1:4-23

WHEN THE END CAME, JESUS TURNED AWAY FROM THE TEMP-tation to be concerned with his physical being. He set his face toward the light of God's presence. "Father, into thy hands I commend my spirit," he whispered. Already he had glimpsed the glory of life as it was to be shared with his heavenly Father.

This message is dramatically pictured in an altar painting by Matthias Grünewald in the chapel in Isenheim, Germany. The altar has double wings which fold over and conceal it. The method of construction offers the artist the opportunity to paint not only the central panel and the interior surface of the open wings, but the exterior surface of the closed wings as well. When we look at the altar in Isenheim when closed, we gaze upon the tragic figure of Christ. He hangs on a rough-hewn cross silhouetted against the darkened sky. The artist has caught the supreme agony of the event in the figure of the Christ and in the faces of the crowd who scorned him. On holy days, however, the altar is opened—and here the artist has pictured a divine miracle. The scenes are not of earth but of heaven. Instead of the darkness of Calvary there is the golden light of the celestial city; in place of the hostile crowd there are shining angels. The artist has visioned the glory of heaven as immediately behind the cross.

The last moments on Calvary showed the concern of Christ for eternity. The time had passed when it mattered what the soldiers did or what the Jewish leaders said. The mind of Jesus was no longer absorbed with the pains which ravaged his body. His thoughts were of God. His physical self had surrendered to the cruel bondage of pain, but his spirit was already reaching out toward an eternal goal.

During the years which followed the Crucifixion, death held no terror for the followers of Christ. They found the pattern for their victory in his words of commitment. Stephen's face was shining as he was stoned. Bishop Polycarp's calmness in the hour of death stirred both the Christians and the pagans in Smyrna. Unnumbered followers of the Galilean marched into the Colosseum in Rome, seeing not the wild beasts which were to tear them to pieces, but the welcoming arms of their heavenly Father.

Centuries later Sir Walter Scott told the story of the triumphant death of Ephraim Macbriar. Captured and condemned to death because of his faith, Macbriar was led through weeping crowds to his execution. "Farewell," he cried, "farewell, farewell! Farewell the world of all delights! Farewell sun, moon, and stars! Welcome God the Father! Welcome sweet Jesus Christ! Welcome blessed spirit! Welcome glory! Welcome eternal life! Welcome death!"

Some Christians sorrow as if they had no faith. Joseph Conrad pictured a scene in which an old seaman lay dead in the bottom of a small boat. "Where is his star now?" asked one of the characters in the drama. "It is out," came the reply, "but who shall miss it from the sky?" Too many of us affirm by our attitudes that the star of life is blotted out in the hour of death, and there is no one to miss it.

Many of us pour lamentations and sorrows upon the body

of a loved one or friend because we have no confidence in the eternal hope. We surround the physical remains with an atmosphere of luxury. We are consumed by grief because we are convinced that the journey is over.

Look yonder at the cross! When life was ebbing away, Christ dismissed his pain-wracked body. His interest and concern were with the part of his being which in the moment of death would be released from the body. He had no fear; no doubts or uncertainties disturbed him. His words throbbed with confident assurance. His spirit belonged to God, and heaven was his natural home.

We bow in silence before the miracle of Calvary. Our lives are different when we turn away from the scene. The focus of life is changed. The Cross enables us to see eternity at the end of our earthly road.

Prayer

Help us, O God, to glimpse the glory of life as it is lived with thee. We want to shape our daily deeds according to thy will. Give us a vision of the eternal life. Save us from the doubts which would darken the end of life with what we know as death. Accept the dedication of what we are and have. Help us to understand the meaning of fellowship with thee, even for eternity. In Jesus' name. Amen.